Frank Lloyd Wright

T0204776

■ Architecture
Collection

UNIVERSITY OF TOLEDO LIBRARIES

Frank Lloyd Wright

Daniel Treiber

E & FN SPON
An Imprint of Chapman & Hall

London · Glasgow · Weinheim · New York · Tokyo · Melbourne · Madras

UNIVERSITY OF TOLEDO LIBRARIES

Published by E & FN Spon, an imprint of Chapman & Hall, 2–6 Boundary Row, London SE1 8HN, UK

Chapman & Hall, 2–6 Boundary Row, London SE1 8HN, UK

Blackie Academic and Professional, Wester Cleddens Road, Bishopbriggs, Glasgow G64 2NZ, UK

Chapman & Hall GmbH, Pappelallee 3, 69469 Weinheim, Germany

Chapman & Hall USA, 115 Fifth Avenue, New York, NY 10003, USA

Chapman & Hall Japan, ITP-Japan, Kyowa Building, 3F, 2-2-1 Hirakawacho, Chiyoda-ku, Tokyo 102, Japan

Chapman & Hall Australia, 102 Dodds Street, South Melbourne, Victoria 3205, Australia

Chapman & Hall India, R. Seshadri, 32 Second Main Road, CIT East, Madras 600 035, India

English language edition 1995

© 1995 E & FN Spon

Original French language edition *Frank Lloyd Wright*, © 1986, Fernand Hazan, Paris

An Autobiography by Frank Lloyd Wright is copyright © The Frank Lloyd Wright Foundation, Scottsdale, Arizona. The quotes which appear here are used with permission. All rights reserved.

Translated by Maggie Rosengarten

Typeset in 11/12.3pt Rockwell by Photoprint, Torquay, Devon
Printed and bound in Hong Kong

ISBN 0 419 20310 9

Apart from any fair dealing for the purposes of research or private study, or criticism or review, as permitted under the UK Copyright Designs and Patents Act, 1988, this publication may not be reproduced, stored, or transmitted, in any form or by any means, without the prior permission in writing of the publishers, or in the case of reprographic reproduction only in accordance with the terms of the licences issued by the Copyright Licensing Agency in the UK, or in accordance with the terms of licences issued by the appropriate Reproduction Rights Organization outside the UK. Enquiries concerning reproduction outside the terms stated here should be sent to the publishers at the London address printed on this page.

The publisher makes no representation, express or implied, with regard to the accuracy of the information contained in this book and cannot accept any legal responsibility or liability for any errors or omissions that may be made.

A catalogue record for this book is available from the British Library

Contents

NA
737
.W7T7413
1995x

Photograph of Frank
Lloyd Wright at
Taliesin, circa 1912–14
(photographer
unknown). Musée
d'Orsay Collection.

A new house

'Water! More water was the cry as more men came over the hills to fight the now roaring sea of devastation. Whipped by the big wind, great clouds of smoke and sparks drove straight down the lengths of Taliesin courts ... I was on the smoking roofs, feet burned, lungs seered, hair and eyebrows gone, thunder rolling as the lightning flashed over the lurid scene ... The destruction had reached to the workrooms – had begun to take hold of them too – water gone, human energy gone ... Suddenly a tremendous pealing roll of thunder and the storm broke with a violent change of wind that rolled the great mass of flame up the valley. It recoiled upon itself once as the rain fell hissing into the roaring furnace.'[1]

This was 1925. The man was a famous Chicago architect, who had been at odds with the establishment for 15 years, and was a voluntary exile in the Wisconsin countryside. Twenty years earlier he had drawn attention to himself by some very sober public buildings and in particular some private houses in a new style, which were extremely unusual but very pleasant to live in.

In 1909, at the age of 40, Frank Lloyd Wright had abandoned his wife, children, home, studio, clientele and respectability and eloped with the wife of a neighbour, Mrs Cheney. After visiting Europe, he finally returned to the valley of his ancestors in Wisconsin and built Taliesin, which was at once a place to live, a studio and an agricultural operation, quite the opposite of the civilized ambience of the elegant suburbs where Wright had lived and worked previously.

In August 1914 Taliesin was ravaged by the first fire, killing seven people including Mrs Cheney.

Wright married the elegant and refined Miriam Noël, and together they spent the period 1915–21 in Japan, where he was building the Imperial Hotel, a commission of grandeur and prestige since the Imperial family was involved in it. There followed two years in Southern California, where he built several houses of vaguely pre-Columbian influence; known as the 'Maya houses', these were less countrified than the 'Prairie houses' he had built in Chicago in the first decade of the century. In 1923 he found himself back in the forefront of the architectural scene, when a dreadful earthquake ravaged Tokyo and the Imperial Hotel alone stood up to the tremors. These years of wandering between Taliesin, Japan and Los Angeles were a time of a difficult emotional relationship: Miriam Noël's mental health was unstable and in time deteriorated; they separated in 1924, one year before the second fire at Taliesin.

Taliesin, a work representative of a whole area of Wright's architectural thinking, is pervaded by an informal harmony of fluidity and architectural pathways, reminiscent of the imperial villa Katsura and

[1] Frank Lloyd Wright, *My Autobiography*, p. 261. Written largely at the end of the twenties (first edition in 1932), *An Autobiography* was republished in 1943, augmented by a fifth book.
The 1943 edition of the autobiography will be our principal travelling companion; it offers invaluable information on the 'subject' Wright, it leaves room for the vision he had in his work, but most of all it provides exceptional insight into his architecture in the making.

Guaranty Building,
Chicago, 1894–5.
Architects: Adler and
Sullivan.

[1] Peter Blake, *Frank Lloyd
Wright: Architecture and
Space*, Baltimore, 1964, p.
85.

[2] 'There may be a gate,
and then a hedge or fence
that forces one to turn, and
then a walk through
gardens, up a few steps
and down a few steps,
more turns through smaller
and larger gardens past
pools, and so forth – until
suddenly a corner of the
building is visible behind
some planting. And only
after the final turn does the
visitor see the building
revealed, more or less in
full. Taliesin East was
designed in exactly that
way – not on paper, not
diagrammatically, but by a
great artist capable of
visualizing a progression of
spaces and forms, a
changing of vistas, a play of
surprises, and of light and
shade from unexpected
sources'. Blake, p. 63.

'HE WILL BE AN ARCHITECT'

[3] Gérard Genette, *Figures
III*, Paris, p. 272.

[4] *Autobiography*, pp. 11,
32.

[5] Wisconsin.

[6] *Autobiography*, p. 55.

the traditional Japanese house. The courtyards which link the buildings, the frequent change in level and the numerous unexpected
views, make Taliesin 'one of the subtlest spatial compositions of our
time' (Peter Blake).[1] As Blake observes, rather than the direct
approach of the classical European tradition the Japanese style
prefers an indirect route consisting of shifts of perspective and
constant surprises.[2] In more than one respect Taliesin echoes the
work of Marcel Proust, a virtual contemporary. An observation made
by Gérard Genette about Proust's great novel *A la recherche du
temps perdu* could apply to Wright's house: 'We must recapture the
sense of incompleteness in this work: the life-giving sense (breath) of
imperfection. The "Recherche" is not a closed object: it is not an
object at all.'[3] A 'Work in progress', Taliesin evolved constantly and
effortlessly never ceasing to modify itself through all the catastrophes,
just as through all the trials and tribulations of everyday life, from 1911
to the end of the thirties when this slow maturation led to a new
Taliesin, in Arizona.

Wright had become an architect at the wish of his mother.[4] After his
father's departure – a decision taken sorrowfully but faced with
composure, as living together had become impossible – the mother
found a position locally for her young son with a cultivated and kindly
Madison civil engineer.[5] In the afternoons he worked with this
engineer and in the mornings he studied civil engineering at the City
University, as the School of Architecture was beyond their means. The
young man enjoyed working in Dean Conover's office, on actual
projects, and in contact with the practical problems of construction.
His fascination was further reinforced when one day 'he was just in
time to hear the indescribable roar of building collapse . . . Whitened
by lime dust as sculpture is white, men with bloody faces came
plunging wildly out of the basement entrance blindly striking out
about their heads with their arms, still fighting off masonry and falling
beams . . . one workman, lime-whitened, too, hung head-downward
from a fifth-story window . . . a ghastly red stream ran from him down
the stone wall.'[6]

Soon frustrated by the lack of scope in the problems tackled by
Conover and more and more moved by the dream of becoming an
architect, Wright made his first decision to leave everything behind:
his mother, his sisters, Dean Conover, the small and quiet provincial
town. When he was eighteen years old he left for Chicago, where he
would at last be able to acquire the necessary experience through
working with a practising architect.

Top: Field Building,
Chicago, 1885–6.
Architect H.H.
Richardson. Bottom:
interior of Chicago
Auditorium, Chicago,
1887–9. Architects
Adler and Sullivan.

After a year with J.L. Silsbee, an architect of the Picturesque school, Wright was taken on by Adler and Sullivan, one of the most prominent avant-garde architectural practices.[1] Sullivan's career was at that time at its peak, his style maturing precisely during the years Wright was in the practice (1887–93). After the Auditorium Building (1887–89), Sullivan built his masterpiece, the Wainwright Building (1890–91), then the Schiller Building (1891–92) on which Wright also worked.

Immediately recognized by Sullivan as an exceptional designer, Wright was an enthusiastic and efficient employee,[2] and was before long put in charge of about thirty draughtsmen.[3] Sullivan showed an uncharacteristic amiability towards his young assistant.

'He loved to talk to me and I would often stay listening, after dark in the offices in the upper stories of the great tower of the Auditorium building looking out over Lake Michigan, or over the lighted city. Sometimes he would keep on talking seeming to have forgotten me – keep on talking until late at night ... And I would catch the last suburban car for Oak Park and go to bed without supper.'[4]

Wright always recognized, even if he did not acknowledge, the influence and affection of the 'Lieber Meister'.[5] To have a master, and a master such as Sullivan, was certainly a piece of good fortune, but as Wright himself pointed out, he for his part was able to understand the revolutionary ideas of his master, without ever failing to exercise the critical intelligence which his prolific reading as an adolescent had sharpened.[6] Sullivan did not introduce Wright to the architectural culture of the time – even before meeting him Wright had acquired a culture comparable to that of the master[7] – but he taught him to think practically, with his daily demands, his insistence on a rigorous discipline of logic and an ethic of a free thinking critical spirit. Wright's already developed 'radical sense of things I had already formed intuitively got great encouragement.'[8]

If prior to 1890 Sullivan was still using the Romanesque style of Richardson for exterior details, around that time Wright saw him finally throwing off the models of the past to develop his own style linked to the expression of the overall logic of the plan. Wright had every day before his eyes the example of a man pursuing a quest as elevated as that of 'the rule so broad as to admit of no exception.'[9] But Sullivan, 'with all his synthesis and logical inclination, his uncompromising search for principle, [he] was an incorrigible romanticist. I have learned to see this as not inconsistent except as the romanticist degenerates to the sentimentalist.'[10]

With Silsbee, Wright had acquired a sound knowledge of the requirements of domestic design. In 1889, thanks to an increase in his salary, he was able to build a small house for himself and his new

[1] 'Radical – going strong on independent lines. Burnham and Root their only rivals.' *Autobiography*, p. 89.

[2] Sullivan's drawings 'were a delight to work upon and work out'. *Autobiography*, p. 97.

[3] *Autobiography*, p. 107.

[4] *Autobiography*, p. 107.

[5] *Autobiography*, p. 92.

[6] 'Now went along these matchless years of master and apprentice. Louis Sullivan, the Master and I, the open-eyed, radical and critical but always willing apprentice.' *Autobiography*, p. 107.

[7] He makes particular note of the fact that Sullivan had no knowledge of the 'Grammar of Ornament' by Owen Jones, a reference work for the avant-garde of the time, for those who supported the 'Arts and Crafts' movement, and for the followers of Viollet-le-Duc (for example Frank Furness, himself a follower of Viollet-le-Duc and Sullivan's teacher).

[8] *Autobiography*, p. 103.

[9] For his part, he said that he could not help but think of the exception which proves the rule. *Autobiography*, p. 107.

[10] *Autobiography*, p. 108.

Charnley house,
Chicago 1891. Frank
Lloyd Wright for Adler
and Sullivan.

[1] 'In this Charnley city-house on Astor Street I first sensed the definitively decorative value of the plain surface, that is to say of the flat plane as such.' *Autobiography*, p. 110.

[2] This was Burnham's opinion, at least. *Autobiography*, p. 126.

[3] '. . . feeling a little nearer to Adler and Sullivan by being there'. *Autobiography*, p. 123.

[4] *Autobiography*, p. 129.

wife. He had met Catherine at a dance – he was 20 and she was 17 – they were married a year later. Adler and Sullivan refused to build private houses, and when out of politeness they were obliged to accept such commissions, Wright was given responsibility for them (outside office hours). He designed and built, under Sullivan's supervision, at least one masterpiece: the Charnley house (1891). 'Neat and straightforward', it was in accord with the great Sullivanian buildings, their requirements and their formal designs: firm and regular articulation of volumes, planes and openings, distinct contrasts between the plain surfaces and the decorative courses.[1]

Then Sullivan discovered that Wright was surreptitiously building houses on his own account (although this was always in his free time). Offended, Sullivan dismissed Wright. The warm and enthusiastic collaboration of six years was followed by a coolness of twelve years during which Wright nevertheless continued to be 'loyal' to Sullivan.[2] Working for himself, Wright began by renting an office on the top floor of the Schiller Building. He had had more involvement in this Sullivan project than in any of his other buildings.[3] For his part, Sullivan retained an interest in the work of his former pupil.[4] Wright always felt profoundly grateful to the 'Master' and was a great comfort to him during the last years when, broken by alcoholism, Sullivan was only the shadow of his former self, forgotten by everyone. Shortly before Sullivan's death, Wright dedicated one of his most inspired projects to him, the 'Glass skyscraper' (1920–24), recognizing that

Interior of the living
room of the Wright
house at Oak Park,
Illinois, 1889.

without Sullivan, without his buildings and his example, he would not
have been able to produce such a 'radical' design.[1] In 1949, Wright's
book *Genius and the Mobocracy*, about Sullivan and his work,
appeared in print.

[1] *Autobiography*, p. 258–59.

OAK PARK 1889

In the new residential suburb of Oak Park, Wright had noticed an old-
fashioned barn with walls clad in vertical boarding, 'honestly
picturesque'.[2] The simplicity of barns no doubt inspired the design of
his own house.

[2] *Autobiography*, p. 80.

   On the front elevation, a gable framing a Serlian motif overhung the
ground floor whose walls undulated with two bow windows. The
wooden clapboards and the brickworks of the terrace walls were in
keeping with the rustic character of the place and did not in any way
detract from the force of the geometric line which, together with the
equilateral triangle of the gable, seemed to respond to the intense
use that Richardson made of the cube and the cylinder or that Sullivan
made of the cube and the square. The two slopes of the roof were
intersected by a cross gable. The severity of this device and the
emphasis on the regular plane owed no doubt more to Richardson
than to Sullivan. At this time Richardson was unanimously considered
the greatest American architect of the century, and Wright would be
familiar with two impressive houses in Chicago itself, where everything, the plan, the volumes, the style, the texture of the walls, was
innovative. These were the Glessner and the McVeagh houses of
1885.[3] The use of the right angle as a leitmotif would become one of
Wright's favourite themes in the 'Prairie houses', as well as another
idea, also present in the 1889 house: the systematic stressing of
horizontal lines.[4] It was not the walls that defined the internal space
but the floor and the shape formed by the ceiling and its cornices.
Four horizontal lines run through the entire house; no vertical is
emphasized. The playroom added in 1893, with its great tunnel vault
lit by a zenithal rooflight and wonderful lamps, maintained the
importance of the horizontal while enriching it with a vertical counter-
point which was to become a major characteristic of Wright's buildings. With this logical principle, interpreted by the hand of the master
– a master who was only 24 years old – and the cruciform volumetric
composition, Wright was already using in 1889–93 the key principles
of the great works of the decade 1900–10.

[3] The Field Building, a
commercial building built
in the same year by
Richardson in Chicago, had
greatly interested Sullivan.

[4] First of all on the interior,
then on both the interior
and the exterior.

   It took a dozen years before these principles he had employed in
the Oak Park house were accepted by his clients. In the first buildings
constructed under his name, Wright's influence was much less appa-
rent than it had been in the building of the vibrant Charnley house.
The clear contrasts, the quality of the ornamentation, seemed often to

Top: Willits house, Highland Park, Illinois, 1901–2. Opposite, bottom: presentation drawing for the H. McCormick house, 1907. Not built.

[1] Mr Moore asked for an 'English house', fearing that he would be ridiculed if he had a house in the Winslow style. 'Could I give him a home in the name of English half-timber good enough so that I would not "sell out"? It was worth trying anyway. I tried it ...' *Autobiography*, p. 129.

have vanished; only the planes remained just as explicit, with a very clear concern with the articulation and the refinements of composition. The best known building from this first period, the Winslow house of 1893, combines a picturesque rear elevation with a Sullivanian front whose 'brutality' caused a scandal, but whose vigour is slightly muted by the enormous subtlety of the decor. The other houses borrowed from this in a clearly eclectic way: the neo-classical and Palladian style for the Blossom house (1892), Richardsonian masses for the Parker house (1892) and the Gale house (1893), half-timbering for the Moore house (1895). The Moore case is interesting: caught between a desire for architectural integrity and the financial necessity of raising three children, Wright risked a compromise: from that time forward he was determined to construct buildings only in conformity with his radical ideas.[1] From 1897 (Heller house) and 1899 (Husser house) a more personal style evolved, with a vigorous organization of masses and a subtle dialectic of volumes and horizontal lines. In 1900, the *Ladies' Home Journal* published two theoretical schemes, one with steep sloping roofs and projecting gables in a peaked-cap shape, the other with shallow roofs in a pavilion style. The first incorporated the familiar bow windows of the period with matching conventional porches and roofs like the bungalows which were very much in vogue at that time in California. Two built projects referred back to this, the Hickox and Bradley houses of 1900. But it was the other type which

PLATE 72 PROJECT: HAROLD McCORMICK HOUSE, LAKE FOREST, ILLINOIS. PERSPECTIVE

Wright developed in almost all of the houses he built in the first decade of the century.[1] Between 1900 and 1909 he built a dozen masterpieces which made him the equal of Horta or Mackintosh, that is to say of the most advanced contemporary European architects. The Willits, Heurtley and Dana houses (1902), the Martin house (1908), the Cheney house (1904), the Coonley house (1907), the Evans, Roberts and Robie houses (1908), are in my opinion the most successful 'Prairie houses'.

[1] The Willits house was the first Prairie house which was 'streamlined . . . Others soon followed in this vein which was now really my own'. *Autobiography*, p. 132.

THE PRAIRIE HOUSE

[2] 'Taking a human being for my scale, I brought the whole house down in height to fit a normal one – ergo, 5' 8½" tall, say. This is my own height . . . It has been said that were I three inches taller than 5' 8½" all my houses would have been quite different in proportion. Probably.' *Autobiography*, p. 141.

'I saw that a little height on the prairie was enough to look much more – every detail as to height becoming intensely significant . . .'[2] A low building with a gently sloping overhanging roof, the Prairie house stretched over the ground, sometimes with outbuildings further accentuating the horizontality. The first floor, of a much lesser area, emerged like a pavilion from the roofs of the ground floor. Large areas of masonry articulated the elevations; expanses of wall often reached only to half the height of the upper floor, leaving a continuous bank of windows running all around under the roof, with the piers of the same height that could if required be used as ventilation shafts between different levels. The ground floor was usually a large flowing space incorporating the various areas of the entrance hall, living room, dining room, etc. Different ceiling heights differentiated and enlivened the different areas of this space. The highest ceiling was often raised on clerestory windows. Large full-height windows captured the mid-season sun. At their feet was a bench for enjoying the view of the garden, with its plant boxes in the foreground raised to the level of the basement wall. At the other end of the room, in a large but sober fireplace, a wood fire crackled. Numerous electric lights added to the golden ambience provided by the sombre wood and the gentle tones of the walls.

The Robie house, one of the best known works of Wright with its streamlined silhouette and its sharp lines, is not only remarkable for its sculptural form but also for the ingenuity of its structure. A linear composition of walls and breast walls form its base and also protect it by creating several courtyards; in summer the volumes of air in the ground floor, in the internal spaces and in the external courtyards serve as reservoirs of coolness. The shady ground floor consists of a rear entrance hall, a billiard room, a children's playroom, service areas and a garage with its forecourt concealed by a high wall. The *piano nobile* consists of two longitudinal volumes, parallel and interesting: at the front are the living rooms, and at the rear, partly extending into the garage forecourt, the servants' wing. Above this

floor and perpendicular to it is the floor for the main bedrooms. All the front walls of the house are set back behind the parapets of the terraces so as to be protected from the summer sun. The projection of the roof of the *piano nobile* on the south side is relatively modest but just sufficient protection when the sun is at its zenith; to the east and to the west, spectacular overhangs provide protection from both the sun and the rain. Inside, the living room and dining room are separated by a fireplace back-to-back with the staircase, but unified by the architectural ceiling and the window wall which runs from one end of the floor to the other. This floor possesses poor heat retention, despite huge masses of brickwork, because more than three-quarters of its perimeter is glazed. All the windows open and are protected by mosquito screens; each one has a radiator of corresponding size, and it even seems that wells were intended to be let into the floor for the installation of small radiators at the foot of each of the French windows which overlook the large front balcony. A complex electric lighting system provides brilliant effects: two longitudinal beams form low-ceilinged 'aisles' either side of the main area, and to these is attached a series of globes, each enclosed in an angular framework, their positions precisely corresponding to the piers and windows of the long elevation; a second series of lights, this time indirect, is concealed behind oak grilles in the beams over the aisles.

The arrangement of the windows is distinctive both in terms of the view and in terms of summer ventilation: in all the Prairie houses,

Main entrance of the
Robie house, situated at
the rear.

diametrically opposite windows could be opened, although they were
sometimes almost inaccessible because they were high up and
behind small galleries – which were very often precursors of the
'architectural promenade'.[1] The double-height areas had the advantage of collecting warm air, which is lighter than cool air: the large
banks of adjoining windows generally opened completely, and on the
opposite side of the room small clerestory windows permitted a
through-draught at the high point, just where the warm air was
concentrated.[2]

Wright had therefore developed a method of designing airy houses,
but in Chicago the problem of heating was just as important as
ventilation, as after the torrid summers come fierce winters.[3] Most
clients could afford to build only using a lightweight construction
system. Wright responded intelligently to this constraint by reducing
heat loss to a minimum, and abandoning the conventional practice
which relied on the thermal capacity of heavyweight masonry to store
heat. The more lightweight a building is, the easier it is to cool down
and heat up quickly, but to do this efficient heating and ventilation are
required. The solution of the summer problem lay in the architectural
arrangement of the volumes and openings. The winter problem was
less significant, as energy was cheap and plentiful – as it had been in
the North of the United States since the Industrial Revolution – and
central heating which used the circulation of hot water had been
developed in the second half of the nineteenth century. Significant
heat losses, of little consequence for comfort in winter, were balanced
by an appreciable gain in comfort in summer. It was therefore not
only pleasant but a logical solution, more than anything else, to
multiply the glazed surfaces which keep thermal capacity low even
in a brick construction, as was the case with a luxury building such
as the Robie house.

Because central heating allowed the house to be successfully
heated whatever its shape, this tended to divide it into more numerous
and smaller elements. The 'box' was one of Wright's *bêtes noires*, not
so much from the point of view of taste but because it seemed to him
absurd to retain an obsolete form if a new one was possible, which
would be at the same time more sensible, more efficient and more
aesthetically pleasing. The house could become a series of delicate
small pavilions, linked to each other by means of galleries or
promenades.

The Coonley house (1907–9) is the finest illustration of the harmony
of pavilions distributed over a delightful garden with a large
pond, with one wing for the bedrooms and another for the servants,
an equally ample gardener's cottage, independent of the actual

[1] In Le Corbusier's words.

[2] Rayner Banham provides
us with the detailed, and no
doubt definitive,
explanation of the
climatology of the Prairie
house. *The architecture of
the well-tempered
environment*, London, 1969,
pp. 104–21.

[3] 'The climate . . . was
violent in extremes of heat
and cold, damp and dry,
dark and bright . . .'.
Autobiography, p. 142.

Opposite, top: Boynton house, Rochester, New York, 1908. Bottom: fireplace at the end of double-height living room of the Roberts house, River Forest, Illinois, 1908. Behind the low wall, the entrance hall and the dining room.

Following double page: living room of the Coonley house, Riverside, Illinois, 1907–9. Top left: original façade. Bottom left: stair wells on both sides of the living room. Top right: modified façade. Bottom right: interior – some of the furniture was designed by Wright.

house but connected to a fourth cruciform building, for the garages and studios. Two wide staircases, on either side of the large living room – which is once again on the first floor – separate it on the one side from the dining room, and on the other side from the bedroom wing. Apparently absurd, these two staircases, emerging on to a blind corridor and lit by superb glazed roofs, facilitate the circulation of air between the *piano nobile* and a very confined ground floor which once again serves as a reservoir of cool air in summer.

Perfecting the rationale of modern living space, the Coonley house was naturally Wright's favourite from the Prairie period. It would have been surpassed only by the McCormick house (1907), if the client had proceeded with the project. The dispersed plan creates shade, multiplies the partitions and allows for an architectural response to the divergences in temperature; it transforms the house set in its garden into an entity of a new kind, into a daily experience wonderful to live in, and which combines the benefits of the indoors with the pleasures of life in the open air.

A new empathy for nature was developing, which led Wright to celebrate, in the middle of the desert, 'that wonderful dining-room sixty miles wide, as long and tall as the universe'[1] for the Ocatillo camp. The architectural emphasis passed from exterior façades to the composition of the interior. The pre-eminence of the interior dictating its form to the exterior promoted a new aesthetic, which was to become more extreme, but which had been evident since the time of the Prairie houses. The austerity of the exterior contrasted with an internal ambience where all the potential of the chosen architectural form was exploited, where the light, from the sides or above, natural or artificial, was treated with extreme care; where the materials were placed in opposition, hot/cold, smooth/rough, natural/artificial and so on. The internal space, the 'void', became more important than the structure.

This characteristic appeared even in houses of modest dimensions, with planes which were inevitably more compact but could nevertheless be striking, with their rigorous formal discipline.[2] The strict symmetry of the planes is not incompatible with the actual experience of a visitor who moves through a fluid space, with continually changing vistas and surprises, and diagonal views which further enhance the sense of space.[3]

Contrary to popular belief, the oldest Prairie houses are not the most symmetrical. The Husser house (1899) and the 1903 plans for the

[1] *Autobiography*, p. 309.

[2] See, for example, the Darton house (Martin annexe of 1903), the Ross house (1906), and the Horner and Evans houses (1908).

[3] '. . . I declared the whole lower floor as one room, cutting off the kitchen as a laboratory . . . Then I screened various portions of the big room for certain domestic purposes like dining, reading, receiving callers . . . The house became more free as space and more liveable too. Interior spaciousness began to dawn.' *Autobiography*, pp. 142–3.

[1] *Autobiography*, p. 309.

[2] Dana (1903), Barton (1904), Beachy (1906), May (1908), Bach (1915), Hollyhock (1920), the Maya houses (1921–4), the Usonian houses for Willey (1934), Winkler-Goetsch (1939), Lewis (1940), Brauner (1943), Boomer (1953), and many others.

[3] *Autobiography*, p. 16.

studio are much more asymmetrical than the Evans, Coonley and Robie houses of 1908–9, not to mention the Coonley Playhouse (1912) which was in the middle of the 'informal' period. In fact, Wright had never 'broken' with symmetry. What he disapproved of was not symmetry, but obtrusive symmetry. 'Here in the wide open spaces (of Arizona), obvious symmetry claims too much, I find, wearies the eye too soon and stultifies the imagination.'[1] He did not condemn symmetry on principle, on the contrary, he often made use of it. Many houses[2] had symmetrically designed gables. Often he established a subtle interplay between an overall asymmetry and fragments which were properly symmetrical; the great domestic creations such as the McCormick design (1907), the Coonley house (1908) or even Hollyhock House (1920) spread out unrestrained over their sites, but made constant use of symmetry and axiality. It was not the overall asymmetry which was striking, but a point of repose supplied by one fragment of the whole, composed of symmetrical volumes and openings with an aura of tranquil nobility.

The architecture of the Prairie house is not, as is often supposed, a set of clever solutions for integrating modern services into a building. In fact, Wright succeeded in reconciling the architectural integrity with necessary technical, mechanical and electrical services in an organism from which no element could be removed without destroying the whole. In his houses, plan and cross-section, lighting, central heating and ventilation, the solid and the void, the overhangs of the roofs and their sloping ceilings, everything worked together as a single mechanism in which no function was performed by a single element and no detail had only one use. According to Wright, in his mother's family 'Unity was their watchword, the sign and symbol that thrilled them, the Unity of all things.'[3] Unity was more than 'total design': a single principle must determine the whole but most important of all that principle must make up a whole from distinct elements, which were heterogeneous and required all the architect's skill to bring them together, from use, construction, space, materials, to ornamentation, the ornament no longer being a minor feature but acting as the catalyst in the fundamental concept of the building.

The Prairie house was a new type of house. It was practical, and one could live in it more comfortably in the face of the elements, it married the useful to the beautiful rather than being a symbol of social status or respectability. Since the end of the eighteenth century and the neo-classical age, the house had been an architectural exercise, and even at the dawn of the industrial age houses were still monuments. It was only after Ruskin and Morris that houses designed by architects actually became homes. Designing his houses with a thoughtful and detailed approach to the control of the domestic environment, that is to say from the point of view of its use, and by thinking of it as a 'machine' – or perhaps rather a 'mechanism' – Wright made 'domesticity' the subject of a serial exercise in the discipline of form, comparable with the work of Palladio or Ledoux. The ordinary dwellings of people were for Wright, as for the other major architects of the early twentieth century, the major architectural problem[1] and the supreme achievement of his art.[2] Wright's inventiveness was not only creative, but also pragmatic, experience constantly modifying and enriching formal essentials, bringing about subtle variations which were always unexpected. Equal in quality to the work of the best European architects of the time, Wright's work was much richer in quantity: the Taliesin Foundation has listed more than 150 buildings which were actually constructed during the first period of his work alone.[3] To consider only the most remarkable of these buildings: none of his contemporaries had the opportunity to construct so many masterpieces in so little time, not even the prolific Edwin Lutyens, whose work, which was traditional and less innovatory, did not possess the same sense of architectural discipline or the astonishing stylistic unity developed by the American between 1900 and 1912.

'This absorbing, consuming phase of my experience as an architect ended about 1909. I had almost reached my fortieth year. Weary, I was losing grip on my work and even my interest in it.'[4] Wright had refined his technique[5] with the Coonley, Evans, Roberts and Robie houses: 'Continuously thrilled by the effort but now it seemed to leave me up against a dead wall . . . Afternoons after four o'clock I had been in the habit of riding Kano, my young black horse (named after the Japanese Master), over the prairies north of Oak Park, sometimes letting him run wild as he loved to do, sometimes reining him in and reading from a book usually carried in my pocket, for I've always loved to read out-of-doors – especially Whitman.'[6] There follows in the autobiography a list of distractions which he enjoyed but which could not succeed in dispelling his boredom,[7] as well as a curious remark concerning the car and the trouble it caused, to him as to everybody else. What Wright does not mention is that a pretty neighbour accompanied him on his drives, the wife of a client for whom he had built a small house in 1904. Wright was attractive; we do not know much about his love life but in 1909 he abandoned his marital home with Mrs Cheney, never to return, like his own father before him.

[1] 'The house of moderate-cost is not only America's major architectural problem but the problem most difficult . . .' *Autobiography*, p. 489, concerning the Usonian houses.

[2] 'The most desirable work of art in modern times is a beautiful living room, or let's say: a beautiful room to live in', *Autobiography*, p. 420.

[3] Taliesin I being number 157 (in 1911, Wright was 42 years old).

THE CRISIS OF 1909

[4] *Autobiography*, p. 162.

[5] During these last years at Oak Park, production consisted of more than ten buildings a year, the number of buildings which were actually constructed far exceeding that of abandoned plans.

[6] *Autobiography*, p. 162.

[7] 'I did not know what I wanted'. *Autobiography*, p. 162.

[1] The portfolio of line drawings was soon followed by a detailed work, illustrated this time by photographs.

[2] For example, he walked the night streets of Paris at 'one of those times of interior anguish'. *Autobiography*, p. 366.

With his new companion Wright went first to Berlin to put the finishing touches to the publication which is now known as the Wasmuth monographs, one of the most beautiful books on architecture the twentieth century has produced.[1] This publication ensured for him lasting fame in Europe and frequent contact with Austrian, German and Dutch avant-garde circles. Unfortunately, the trip to Europe was not completely happy;[2] in 1911 Wright and Mrs Cheney returned to Chicago.

THE FOUR WOMEN

[3] Hillside Home School (1902).

[4] *Autobiography*, p. 262.

[5] *Autobiography*, p. 275.

[6] Built in the Price tower (1952–6).

[7] Actually constructed in the Morris shop (1948), the Guggenheim Museum (1943–58), the Friedman and David Wright houses (1950) and the Llewellyn Wright house (1953).

After the break of 1909, which was both conjugal and social, the true companion of the architect could only be the one he would make with his own hands, his house. In a very intimate relationship, they would breathe with one and the same breath.

Each subsequent rupture in his love life would coincide with a fire, each new departure with a reconstruction. In 1911, on a plot of land which his mother gave him, close to the buildings he had constructed a few years earlier for his Lloyd-Jones aunts,[3] Wright started to build 'Taliesin'. Its destruction by fire in 1914 took with it Mrs Cheney, and led to the entrance of the third woman in his life, Miriam Noël, who sent him a message of sympathy after the tragedy. In turn the end of his relationship with her coincided with a new fire, a new reconstruction, a new meeting. The second fire of 1925 half destroyed Taliesin but this time Wright immediately and confidently began rebuilding. 'But Taliesin lived wherever I stood. A figure crept forward to me, out of the shadows, to say this. And I had believed what Olgivanna said.'[4] Wright was no doubt correct in considering this almost spiritual apparition so important. In her he met the companion he had been waiting for, basking in the prestige of the ancient European aristocracy.[5] A personality sufficiently similar to his own to be accepted, but strong enough not to be crushed, Olgivanna would be the competent manager, on whom he could lean in order to continue his work during the very hard times that the world was about to pass through.

From 1925 unashamedly modernist designs became more numerous, with, during the first years of living with Olgivanna, exceptional richness of invention. They would be endlessly taken up again and reworked during the 25 years which followed, until the opportunity arose for them to be actually built. The first versions of the Glass Skyscraper date from 1921 and 1924,[6] the first use of the regular plan grids date from the Maya houses; the first circular sketches of the Gordon Strong Automobile Objective and Planetarium are from 1926,[7]

Top: Barton house,
annexe of the Martin
house, 1903. Bottom:
plans for the Ross
house, Lake Delavan,
Wisconsin, 1902.

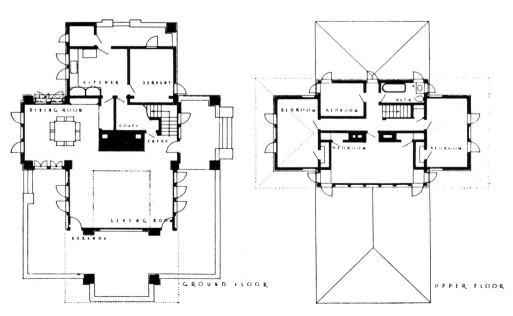

GROUND FLOOR

UPPER FLOOR

Johnson Wax Company, Racine, Wisconsin, 1936–50. Publicity department reception area.

[1] In the Beth Sholom synagogue (1954).

[2] Developed in Taliesin West (1938).

[3] 'Usony' is the name invented by Samuel Butler to designate an ideal America.

[4] In my opinion the Morris shop (1948), the Friedman house (1950) and the Price Senior house (1955).

[5] In his last building, when he was an old man (between eighty and ninety years of age), he continually went back over the 'styles' of earlier periods.

but the enriched finishing touches as well as the Steel Cathedral of 1926[1] and the desert projects of 1927[2] came after the meeting with Olgivanna. If she was not the inspiration of this work, the emotional security she gave Wright certainly helped him to bring his later work to fruition.

After the modernist prototypes of 1929–31 (the Lloyd-Jones house, the House on the Mesa, Saint Mark's Tower) Wright was to invent a new type of house, the 'Usonian'[3] house, deriving from the Prairie house and exemplified by a number of buildings. In 1936, at the age of 67, Wright produced his two best-known creations, 'Fallingwater' and the Johnson Wax Building, whose spectacular modernity left nothing to envy in the European avant-garde. It has been fashionable to denigrate the Usonian houses – and even more Wright's post-1950 buildings – at the same time as praising the Oak Park period. On analysis, this criticism does not hold. After the great Usonian classics, particularly around the year 1940, Wright produced new works, returning to a more formal language, and with a genius just as sure as in the masterpieces of 1908, 1923 and 1936.[4] Moreover, many early buildings were not absolute successes: the Florida Southern College buildings (1938–41) do not, to me, possess Wright's usual grace; even during the Chicago years, the quality of his work was erratic.

'The Woman' is a rare character in the 'Lives of the Great Architects'. Confined to a supporting role, she does not illuminate the biography of the architect as she does that of the poet. Wright is an exception to this rule. From his first marriage in 1890 to his death in 1959, Wright's life can be divided into four periods each characterized by a female companion: Catherine (1890–1909), Mrs Cheney (1909–14), Miriam Noël (1915–24), Olgivanna (1925–59). This division does not necessarily signify a causal relationship between the woman and architectural work, but a symbolic one – the companion only lends her name to a period of time – which gives perspective to the historian's analysis. This analysis tends to concentrate on the first and the last of the four women because they coincided with landmarks in the history of architecture. What happened between these two major periods (1900–8 and 1936–40), and what happened afterwards,[5] is conveniently overlooked.

In complete contrast to the simple, smooth and asymmetrical volumes on which modernism is based (or so it is supposed), we see in this period more and more rigid composition (even to the point of using the strictest symmetry) and excess of ornamentation which

pervades and even distorts the structure. This side of Wright has been marginalized by history, dismissed as obscure aberrations which are accounted for by a theory of regression, or by Wright's supposed 'mystery'. A neat concept of historical progression would suggest that having been a precursor, Wright developed into the most brilliant modern architect – but his work defies this. His achievements were effected by means of advances and regressions within a complex creativity, regardless of the principles of chronological progression and of the classical development of modern architecture.

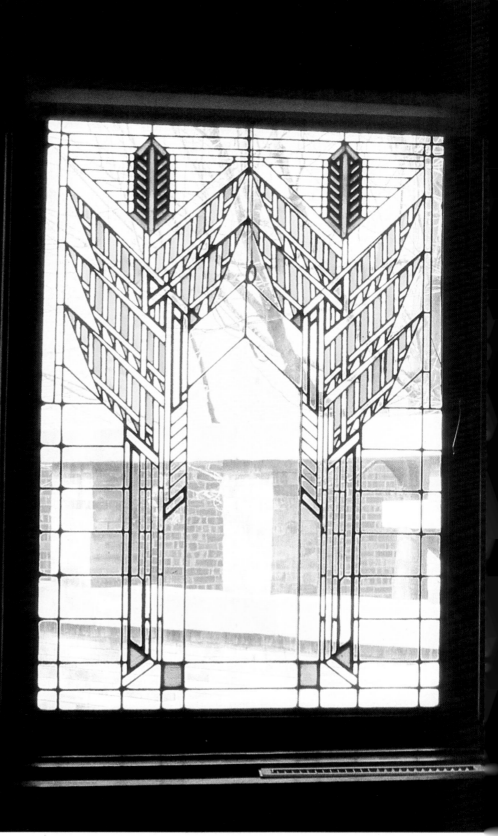

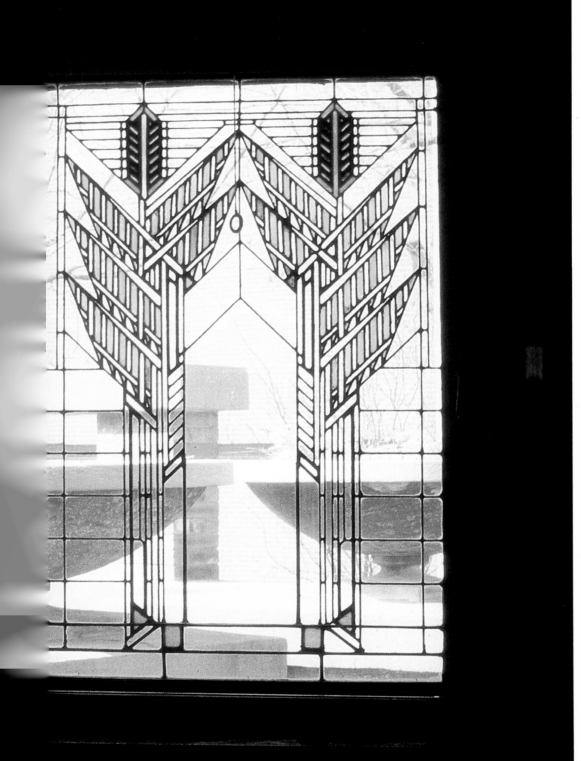

A modern project

Top: design for Yahara Boat Club, Madison, University of Wisconsin, 1902, Wasmuth file 1910. Bottom: Hillside Home School, Spring Green, Wisconsin, 1902, later integrated into Taliesin.

Among the public buildings which Wright designed during the Chicago period, three projects stand out clearly: the Yahara Boat Club of 1902, the Larkin Building of 1904 and the Unity Temple of 1906. The Yahara Club was not built, but the section shown in the Wasmuth monographs is one of the favourite proofs for Wright's 'premonitory modernism'. However neither the ritualistic symmetry of this public building, which was somewhat ceremonious for a boating club, nor in particular the forward breaks at the corners, an entirely classical device, was 'modernist'. In Wright's design, the reinforcement of the corners was strictly visual; it was in fact an articulation of solid volumes, sympathetic with the classical spirit, in which the 'central block', the periphery, the corner, etc. each played a distinct role. Particularly strongly in the other buildings of 1902–4, such as the Hillside Home School or the Dana, Little and Martin houses, Wright's articulation of volumes is a matter of topology rather than of internal function.

In the Unity Temple and the Larkin Building on the other hand, the volumes become more or less separated by deep incisions or even by a straightforward extrusion outside the basic perimeter of the building, the volumes corresponding to the various elements of the plan. The overall form of the Unity Temple is entirely achieved by the articulation of its elements: first of all the two parts of the building – the auditorium and the Sunday school – are treated as separate entities each with their own block, connected by the entrance hall. The constituent elements of each block are in their turn disassociated, differentiated and positioned in hierarchical order: the main volume is in each case a central cube, with the corners detached from it and projecting porticoes, on two sides in the case of the school and on four in that of the auditorium. Solid corners and symmetrical masses also control the Millard and Storer Maya houses, whereas the Freeman house made an innovative reversal: the solid corners metamorphosed into angles of glass whose immateriality was accentuated by the omission of the mullion of the corner, and which anticipated the famous vertical glass window of Fallingwater (1936). Even in the fluid space of the Usonian houses, the articulation, the solid corners and the combination of slabs, balconies and piers is sometimes as solid as in the Unity Temple, although they no longer control any more than a fragment of the building.[1] Wright liked to quote Sullivan's words: 'take care of the terminals and the rest will take care of itself'.[2] A problem inevitably arises at the junction of two materials but for Wright as for Sullivan, the question was more general, it concerned the entire architectural discipline.[3]

[1] For example, the Willey house (1934), the Goetsch-Winkler house (1939), the Lloyd-Lewis house (1940) or the Brauner house (1943).

[2] Bruce Brooks Pfeiffer, catalogue 'F.L. Wright Drawings' Max Protech/G.A. (Ill.10), Tokyo 1984.

[3] Wright compares the discipline of a plan to the grammar of a language. The natural house (New York, 1954), pp. 181–3.

GEDRUCKT UND VERLEGT VON ERNST WASMUTH A.-G., BERLIN

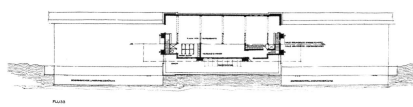

FLUSS

STRAIGHT LINE AND FLAT PLANE

[1] Note the indicative presence of squares. Wright would use the square all through his life as a signature on his drawings. It was also the shape of the Japanese covers which he liked to use or simulate, for example on the façade of the Morris shop.

[2] *Autobiography*, p. 157.

[3] *Autobiography*, p. 110, concerning the Charnley house.

[4] 'Keep the straight lines clean ... the flat plane expressive ... but let texture come into them ...'. *Autobiography*, p. 157.

[5] *Autobiography*, p. 146.

[6] 'A smooth untouched sheet of fine paper is one of the fairest of sights'. *Autobiography*, p. 95.

[7] 'To cut into the walls is an act of violence', F.L. Wright, *The future of architecture*, New York 1953 and Paris 1966 (p. 131).

The quality which earned the Yahara Boat Club its place in the history of modern architecture was its absence of ornamentation, which was worthy of a Loos. But there were other features for which it was equally remarkable: the very Sullivanian emphasis of the offset horizontal slab – which was present in all Sullivan's classics and also in the Unity Temple – and especially the sharp divisions which broke up the wall vertically into five parallel strata and which contrasted with the straight unbroken line of the roof slab. Narrower than the building, the slab accentuated the impression of delicacy, lightness and movement, as well as an unreal, dream-like quality. Unlike the Prairie houses, no conventional material or form interfered with the pure composition of abstract planes and straight lines.[1] Nevertheless, the houses, just like the public buildings, were regulated by the 'language of the straight line and the flat plane',[2] whether it was a question of 'plain'[3] surface or 'textured' surface as would be the case in Los Angeles around 1922.[4] From the first Prairie houses, Wright took up 'the streamline and the plain surface seen as the flat plane'.[5] His abstract compositions were always contrapuntal: if the overall form was horizontal, it was imparted rhythm by the verticals – and reciprocally – nevertheless, always with a powerful emphasis on the dominant line. The horizontal was stressed repeatedly in the Yahara Boat Club and the Robie house and the same was true of the vertical in the Larkin building.

In his account of his first experiences in Sullivan's practice, Wright gives us an insight into his character: preparing his drawing board, he took great delight in the white surface of the paper.[6] For someone with this sensitivity to the pure plane surface, to pierce openings in a wall was very difficult. Although in many instances the openings are pushed out to the edges of the walls, there were still many times when the masonry of the façade had to be torn open.[7] His windows are seldom mere punctured holes; rather they gather around themselves a complex ornament which might even structure the whole wall. From the Winslow house of 1893 onwards, Wright was surrounding the ground floor openings with a scrolling pattern like a Greek key. He took up the idea of the frame again in some of the windows of the Imperial Hotel, once more treating it with vigour, although it was at the same time ingeniously revolutionized. In other buildings, the windows are drawn on the walls like architectural ideograms, their dislocated components tied together by string courses, slabs, plant boxes or heavy piers which give them the impression of extra thickness. Around the edge of the orifice, the wall might sprout lips, like a geometrical, almost script-like swelling of the skin.

When Wright was working with Sullivan 'From the very beginning

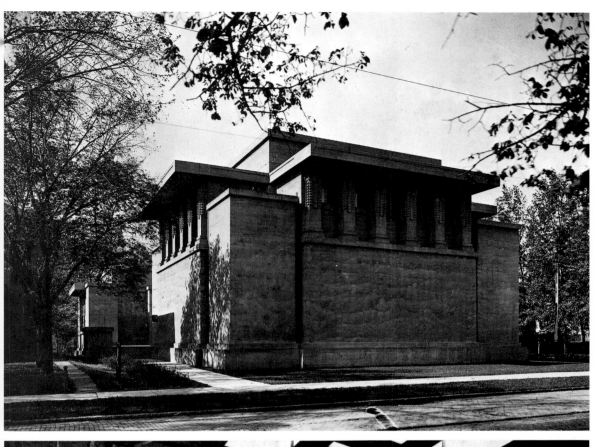

my T-Square and triangle were easy media of expression for my geometrical sense of things. But, at the time, Sullivanian ornament was efflorescence pure and simple ... whenever the Master would rely upon me for a detail I would mingle his sensuous efflorescence with some geometric design, because, I suppose, I could do nothing else so well. And, too, that way of working to me seemed to hold the surface, give needed contrast, be more architectural.'[1]

From large areas of plants, grass and leaves inextricably intertwined to infinity, Wright brought ornament – and design – towards something more modern and with more architectural discipline. For Wright, the straight line and knotwork were not in conflict; on the contrary they responded to one another. The autobiography begins with a 'Prelude', a story: a little boy and his uncle walking over countryside dusted with snow; the child escapes and runs to gather on one side and then the other a bouquet of frozen flowers. 'The lesson was to come. Back there was the long, straight, mindful, heedless line Uncle John's own feet had purposefully made. He pointed to it with pride. And there was the wavering, searching, heedful line embroidering the straight one like some free, engaging vine as it ran back and forth across it. He pointed to that too – with gentle reproof.'[2] A few pages further on, Wright interprets the story: 'These valley-folk feared beauty, seeing in it a probable snare for unwary feet, and

[1] *Autobiography*, p. 104.

[2] *Autobiography*, p. 3.

Evans house, Chicago,
1908.

making the straight way their own feet might mark in the snow less
admirable in their own sight and as an example for irresponsible
youth.'[1]

[1] *Autobiography*, p. 16.

FORMAL DISCIPLINE

The Prairie houses were of two types: they were either broken up
into a collection of pavilions linked to a greater or lesser degree, or
their spaces were assembled into a fairly compact volume with a
cruciform plan. The Willits house, its various rooms extending from a
triple central fireplace, represented the latter type, whereas the
Coonley house was definitely the best illustration of the 'pavilions'
arrangement. The Evans house (1908) is a smaller building, combining
a longitudinal silhouette (like the Robie house) with a central square
mass, symmetrical around both axes except where relieved by a
slight variation on one corner. On a reduced scale the 'terminals'
dominated the plan with articulations between walls, corners and
windows. Prairie houses were regularly built on this smaller scale.
The Martin house (1904) was of the 'pavilion' type with its expansive
footprint, but its plan possessed an unusual number of 'pivots' which
clarified the conceptual layout, defined by eight small square units in
which radiators were concealed behind bookcases surmounted by
small windows. This type of plan has been frequently commented on.[2]
The regulating layout consists of two irregular grids of straight lines
intersecting to create symmetrical 'matrices' (Castex-Panerei). This
'tartan' (MacCormac) regulates both the interior and the peripheral
areas such as porches, paved terraces, staircases, flower boxes and
other flower beds.

[2] For example, by J. Castex and Ph. Panerai or R. MacCormac.

In the four Maya houses in Los Angeles, the 'tartan' was metamorphosed into a regular grid 'organically' linked to the construction. This
followed from the method of assembly of the concrete 'textile blocks',
which were all of the same size and shape.[3] The framework was found
again in the 'modernist' Lloyd-Jones house (1929) and in other later
houses built of concrete blocks. It also appeared in a number of
Usonian houses of which the classic examples came from 1939–40, all
designed on frameworks of squares marrying construction and
morphology.[4] In contrast, the main building of San Marcos-in-the-
Desert (1927) was designed on a triangular-based framework. For
some Usonian houses Wright returned to this framework and combinations of the equilateral triangle such as the hexagon or the
lozenge, and more rarely the octagon, which combines triangle and
square.[5] Based on lozenge frameworks, the Wall house (1941), the
Clinton Walker house (1949), the Boomer house (1953) and others had
triangular or hexagonal living rooms superimposed on the framework

[3] Although there were sometimes variations, in particular of the corners or the 'batters'.

[4] The Pauson, Sturges, Winckler-Goetsch, Pew houses . . .

[5] Nevertheless, the Leigh-Stevens ranch (1940) and the Vigo Sundt house (1942) for example return to this idea.

Presentation drawing
for the E. Stone house,
1906. Not built.
Opposite, bottom: detail
of the playhouse of the
A. Coonley house, 1912.

[1] 'Freedom is the title and
the graph of this book but
there is this to
acknowledge: there is no
such thing in itself . . . The
only freedom we have a
right to ask is the freedom
to see – to be – to believe
– and to love the beautiful
as our souls conceive it,
perceive it or as we can
feel it. That freedom is the
only freedom for men. And
it is freedom enough. It is
Our Country.'
Autobiography, p. 377.

like a palimpsest. The frameworks were never rigidly adhered to.
Sometimes, a wall was added to the framework: but it was only a tool
to guide the hand without hindering it. Discipline does not conflict with
freedom,[1] it organizes and stimulates creation: through the richness
of possible combinations, substitutions and alternatives which progress logically one from another, it opens new possibilities for the
creator at each step.

During the forties, the figure of the circle became more dominant.
Sometimes, circular forms were regularly distributed on a rectilinear
layout (Loeb house, 1942) but in general there was a juxtaposition of
circles of different sizes (from the Jester plan of 1938 onwards),
intersecting circles (Friedman house, 1950) or circular segments

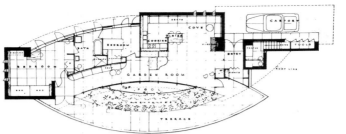

Left: plan for the Laurent house, Rockford, Illinois, 1949–52. Opposite, top: Ann Pfeiffer chapel, Florida Southern College, Lakeland, Florida, 1939–40. Bottom: Kalita Humphrey Theater, Dallas, Texas, 1955.

(David Wright house, 1950). The house for another of Wright's sons, Llewellyn, combined almond shapes with wider curves. Although few were built, some of the designs for public buildings used the same variations on the circle (a car park for Pittsburgh or the Huntingdon Hartford club, of 1947). Paradoxically it was the spiral, the extension of the circle, which was the basis of a number of designs that were actually built, such as the Morris gift shop (1948) and the Guggenheim Museum (1943–59).

GEOMETRIC ASSEMBLIES

In the frameworks based on the triangle, the lozenge and, indeed, the circle, Wright seems to be substituting these shapes directly for the square. But the primary shapes of geometry can also be juxtaposed. The pure system, based on a single shape used on several scales, is distinguishable from the combined system which used different geometrical shapes. Wright explored the two techniques in detail, the pure system first, progressing to the other.[1] Some of his early work can also be interpreted as associations of dissimilar volumes, such as the Naloma Country Club of 1924, the Glasner house (1905), the Cooper design (1890), or even 'Romeo and Juliet', a windmill whose plan combined a circle and a lozenge, and which was built in 1895 on the Lloyd-Jones land, near to the site of the future Taliesin. All these were juxtapositions on the horizontal plane, but the first designs for the Morris house (1946), and the administration 'tower' of the Guggenheim, freely superimposed basic geometrical forms on a vertical plane.

Wright first encountered the 'jeu' or play element in artistic technique at the same time as he acquired an idea of formal discipline, when his mother brought back a set of Friedrich Froebel teaching games from the Centennial Exhibition in Philadelphia in 1876.[2] The German educationalist advocated learning through play, developing the imagination through games which were often very simple. These gave Wright a knowledge of various geometrical applications, the experience and the taste for formal exploration – especially concerning articulation, hierarchy and substitution – as well as the sense of imagination, since the system provided in its operational rules a place for the most absolute fantasy, the artist's vision. Froebel's games consisted not only of the famous cubes but also of squares, spheres, string and folded paper. Wright used the technique of folding, for example, when confronted with the problem of bringing out a dominant line in complicated spatial compositions such as the dining room in the Imperial Hotel, and the First Unitarian Church.

[1] As for the Laurent house (1952). An example of Wright's imagination and freedom, the Laurent house is made up of the intersection of concentric circles which form among other things an almond-shaped terrace, and of a series of cuboid rooms, broken by minuscule openings.

[2] *Autobiography*, p. 13.

THE KALITA HUMPHREYS THEATER

THE LAYER

[1] In particular in the
extension to the Studio
(1895) and in the Husser
house (1899).

[2] The stone (the building)
'flung long arms in any
direction'. *Autobiography*,
p. 170.

It was Taliesin, perhaps because of its repeated redesigns, in which
the 'tartan' was superseded by what might be referred to as the
Usonian geometry. Its informal composition descended, by way of the
Prairie houses, from the more fluid pre-1900 designs which were
composed of parallels and orthogonal counterpoints derived directly
from the Queen Anne style. In fact before developing the Prairie
house Wright performed a critical analysis of the Queen Anne house
and explored the same 'picturesque' logic as the principal masters of
the style, Norman Shaw and H.H. Richardson.[1] Wright's 'tartan' came
from the traditional method of practice in which the architect produces the definitive design, and that is how the finished building will
look. The flexible approach of Taliesin, on the other hand, was
singularly well suited to a slow maturation, with its 'changes of tack',
its impromptu extensions and the radical changes which the fires
brought about. Because of its rambling nature Taliesin was in a state
of permanent evolution, always open to modifications. It sent out
runners like a strawberry plant.[2] The slightest thickening at the end
of a wall, at the end of a straight line flung out into the landscape,
could be developed into a new organism growing in accordance with
the same rule as the principal masses from which it emanated. It was
enough to transform the thickening into a small shelter, with its points
of support, its little pavilion roof, its infill wall broken by a door
embellished with smaller lateral openings ... and the little shelter,
which might hardly have room to hide a bench, a jardiniere or a few
rakes became the worthy offspring of the initial structure. A retaining
wall, or even a border between gravel and lawn, was likely to suggest
to Wright the possibility of throwing out a new offshoot, each time
further into the countryside.

SYMMETRY
AND THE PATH

[3] One might almost say
that it is made, at least the
central part, of the
juxtaposition of three
gigantic Prairie houses: the
first for the main entrance
hall (with the restaurant and
the two 'bridges'
connecting with the wings),
a second on the first floor
(with the auditorium and
the great lateral
promenades), and finally a
third, above, for the great
banqueting hall.

The Cutten and Booth houses of 1911, contemporaries of the first
Taliesin, and then 'Northome' for Francis Little (1913) and 'Hollyhock
House' for Aline Barnsdall (1920), have the most liberated plans, but
these were greatly surpassed by Taliesin III, which was built from
1925 onwards. Paradoxically, the most significant works of this
decade, Midway Gardens and the Imperial Hotel, in spite of their
sculptural dynamism, are composed on strictly symmetrical plans.

The Imperial Hotel in Tokyo uses the cruciform plan of the Prairie
house[3] but more particularly makes use of an effective combination
of storey heights: the cross can have at its centre either a very high-
ceilinged space (as in the lobby and the dining room), or a low space,
as in the spacious lateral 'promenade'. Adjacent to this low-ceilinged
area, the 'parlour' is the pivot of the overall composition; it is on the
building's main axis of symmetry, along with the entrance halls at

Imperial Hotel, Tokyo, 1914–21. Top left: 'promenade' linking the halls to the two bedroom wings; on the mezzanine, the foyer of the auditorium. Furniture designed by Wright. Top right: masonry detail.

Bottom: view of the courtyards between the north bedroom wing, on the right, and the central halls.

either end and the three other principal areas. But the visitor walking through the hotel cannot stay on this axis. He enters the main entrance courtyard beneath a canopy on one of the paths either side of the pool on the central axis, and he joins the axis only at the entrance porch; and then once inside he is obliged to skirt around the double-height dining room. In contrast to the Beaux Arts idea, the path through the building modifies the symmetry of the composition; it plays with it, twists itself around the central axis like the interlacing that the young Wright traced in the snow around the 'straight path' of his uncle.

To these convolutions are added ascents and descents, vistas of the garden courts and the surprise effects of space and light. Obstacles and clear straights, bottlenecks and open spaces: *rallentando* and *accelerando*; Wright modelled the path like a racing driver or a musician, composing an epic work in harmony with the city,[1] recreating a universe which provides a landscape setting for every feature of the building. The wings which enclose the hotel's 'outside' spaces create a more acceptable setting than the neighbouring buildings, which are appalling examples of European academic architecture of the time. In an equally real fashion the hotel transforms its various components into an artificial landscape, inhabited by organic forms and petrified waterfalls. From the entrance lobby, the nearest spaces, to use a domestic equivalent, are like rugs at the side of the imposing mountain which is the central block.

The years he spent in Japan while the hotel was under construction, after his initial visit in 1906, gave Wright the opportunity to acquire a deeper understanding of Japanese thinking and art, which would further refine the Japanese influence which is often attributed to the Prairie houses: organization of interior space into areas which are more or less partitioned, emphasis on the horizontal, subdivision of walls into panels, a sympathetic relationship between the house, with its large, shallow-pitched roof and its garden, and the countryside. Historians agree in placing Wright's first encounter with Japan around 1893, on the occasion of the Chicago World's Fair where a half-size model of a Japanese temple was exhibited. But the Japanese influence should no doubt be sought elsewhere, in his 'first Japanese print',[2] in this 'most exquisite art on earth'[3] which 'the gospel of the elimination of the insignificant' had acquainted him with,[4] and on which he wrote an essay.[5] To ascribe the Japanese influence to Japanese prints is in fact highly plausible if one considers the circulation and more particularly the impact of these woodcuts on Western artistic milieux well before 1890, in fact from the 1860s onward. In Tokyo Wright was totally aware of the cultural invasion which Japan was experiencing: he wanted to make the Japanese aware of the inherent qualities of

[1] 'The fascinating mystery of Tokio was all around us. Tokio is very much like London in many respects. There is so much room in it for surprises. A dingy street outside, palaces immediately within the humble street doors. Casual gates and quiet entrance ways.' *Autobiography*, p. 204.

[2] *Autobiography*, p. 205.

[3] *Autobiography*, p. 326.

[4] *Autobiography*, p. 204.

[5] The Japanese Print, an interpretation (1912).

Imperial Hotel, Tokyo.
Entrance known as 'The
Emperor Entrance'. In
the foreground the low
walls of the courtyard
pond.

Opposite: Imperial Hotel, Tokyo, 1914–21. Soffit of an overhang. Page 58: Barnsdall 'Hollyhock' house, 1917–21. Top: living room; bottom: pond and amphitheatre-style garden. Page 59: texture wall of the Millard house, Pasadena, California, 1921–3.

Page 60: transparency in the banqueting hall of the Ennis house, Los Angeles, 1913. Page 61: top, 'textile block' from the Freeman house, Los Angeles, 1922–4; bottom, 'textile block' from the Millard house.

Page 62: corner detail from the Freeman house. Page 63, top: plateaux of the Kaufmann house, 1936–7. In the background the guest house. Page 63, bottom, an internal corridor in the Johnson Wax building.

[1] See the article devoted to Wright in *Japan Architect* 11/12 of 1984, pp. 94–6.

their own architectural tradition, a tradition which he himself admired enormously but which the wave of occidentalism of the Meiji era had devalued in the eyes of the Japanese. For Wright the hotel should be neither American nor Japanese, but a free interpretation of the Oriental spirit, which could help Japan create a new living environment for an equally new life.[1]

MODERNISM

[2] *Autobiography*, p. 336.

[3] *Autobiography*, p. 377.

[4] *Autobiography*, p. 359.

[5] 'The engineers are quite often as silly as architects. I have seen that experts can be "wrong for more than fifty years".' *Autobiography*, p. 310.

[6] *Autobiography*, p. 52.

[7] *Autobiography*, p. 150.

[8] *Autobiography*, p. 126.

The ornamentation of the Imperial Hotel and the traditional forms of its roofs might be surprising since Wright never ceased to affirm that it was absolutely necessary to produce architecture in keeping with our time, to '[make] architecture again natural to our way of life in this twentieth century,'[2] to write 'this keen new romance of Time, Place and Man I have called modern'.[3] Like other moderns, Wright thought that the century had dawned with 'the honest engineering architecture',[4] even if subsequently it came up against the dullness of routine.[5] As a student he had been unable to afford to study at the School of Architecture, so he had been spared 'the curse of the "architectural" education of that day'.[6] He saw neo-classicism unfurl over the United States with its 'meaningless elaboration . . . the United States were being swept into one grand rubbish heap of the acknowledged styles, instead of intelligently and patiently creating a new architecture'.[7] When, after success of the Winslow house, Daniel H. Burnham, the former associate of John Root, wanted to send Wright to Paris and Rome for six years of academic studies, all costs paid, Wright refused. In a revealing way, Wright called upon the spirit of Sullivan, Root and Richardson to affirm his faith in the spirit of modernism. To return to the rules of the ancient Greeks seemed to him contrary to the truth, contrary to what could be truly American, for Wright indeed saw the modern search as a question of the 'here and now'.[8]

Wright answered the two versions of the past that dominated the institutions of America at the turn of the century – the British tradition and Graeco-Roman art – by offering two voices of his own, sometimes both simultaneously: one was a new idiolect, close to that of Sullivan but also to that of the Viennese Secession, and already modernist; the other was the language of a past that had no academic respectability, the language of pre-Columbian America, divided between South (Maya) and North (wigwams). Unlike most of the innovative architects of the twentieth century, Frank Lloyd Wright did not reject the past but evoked his own fantasy of it, in a way which was at once literal and free, that is to say in conformity with the code of fantasy. There was refashioning, manipulation, inventing, but never unqualified acceptance of traditional values. His neo-Indian primitivism has often

Kaufmann house, 1936–7, side staircase.

Page 66: Larkin Building, Buffalo, New York, 1903–4. Page 67: Richard Lloyd-Jones house, 'Westhope', Tulsa, Oklahoma, 1929.

been interpreted as an attempt to anchor the present in an American past,[1] his own writings in no way support this. In fact, with the introduction of these forms and ideas, he broke entirely new ground through rejection of the styles which were then in vogue in the United States and which had been imported from Europe: namely classicism and modernism.

[1] In particular by Vincent Scully.

By constant renewal, Wright's work even juxtaposes contrary and incompatible theories; its coherence is not stylistic but critical: it is defined by the very past that it opposes. As it opposes more than one existing language, several discourses, including traditional values and fashionable ideas, may be countered at the same time. Suppose that the architect's work exists on four levels: technical, semantic, functional and sculptural. This enables the classification of a number of features, if only provisionally. Technical examples include the cantilever with which Wright was fond of replacing the post-and-lintel combination; the mushroom pillar; the folded-paper structure; the shell, or even the external cage structure of the Sullivan tower, was replaced in the skyscraper designs of the 1920s by a central structural column supporting cantilevered floors. Semantic examples include his opposition to the 'traditional' house, the pseudo-Romanesque or pseudo-Gothic church, and all those essentialist aberrations of which the gingerbread house is the ultimate example. Functional examples include the organization of the interior spaces of the house, or even the 'human scale', the slapstick element of decorous modernism.[2] Finally, as to sculptural examples, Wright turned his back on three aspects of the art: English cottage style, Graeco-Roman academicism, and functionalistic internationalism. When the International Style began to be discussed, Wright often referred to the drawings of the Larkin Building,[3] which represented for him the beginning of real modern architecture, creating new forms and a new space instead of an outworn norm, 'an affirmative negation' which was a denial of the insincere use of materials, excessive decoration, and the building-as-box.

PARADOX

[2] Peter Blake remarks that in the Imperial Hotel, the door handles were often placed so high up that the little Japanese maids could only reach them by standing on tip-toe: 'As Wright liked the grace of Japanese women, this was possibly done intentionally'. Blake, p. 70.

[3] B.B. Pfeiffer, p. 6.

This critical attitude was probably what differentiated Wright from his most recent 'disciples'. They adopt his designs or make a pastiche of them by filling the gaps with a medley which is easily improvised from such a varied style. Far from opposing conventionality, they stick to an introverted idiolect. This attitude is the exact opposite of Wright's heterodoxical criticism: it merely follows the exemplar not in order to counter it but to honour it. Although Wright was fond of presenting himself as a misfit,[4] a rebel who was frequently denied planning permission, his conflict was not simply

[4] *Autobiography*, p. 16.

for the sake of conflict: 'There is an important difference between the merely "experimental" and a genuine experiment. The one may be a feeling for novelty. The other is rationally based upon experience seeking a better way.'[1]

Wright was self-educated; as a child he read widely, as a student more so.[2] Life on the farm had confirmed his sense of pragmatic experimentation; the architect's life would familiarize him with 'this marvellous book-of-books, Experience'.[3] 'Ever since I can remember trying to build, tests have been going on under my supervision . . . The supreme test, I suppose, was the earthquake's grasp of the Imperial Hotel . . . the building process extending back over a period of forty-five years resembles the continuous test to which life itself subjects the architect himself.'[4]

To this reference to the Imperial Hotel we should add the famous account of the specimen 'dendriform shaft' of the Johnson Wax Building.[5]

The liberal use of ornament in Wright's architecture, despite the slogan of Adolph Loos, 'Ornament is crime', which was unanimously adopted by the European modernist architects at least during the inter-war period, in fact raises the issue of the machine. In a lecture in 1901, 'The Arts and Crafts of the Machine', Wright represented the machine as a tool for the artist.[6] In this he was contradicting the

[1] *Autobiography*, p. 471.

[2] Carlyle, Plutarch, Ruskin, William Morris, Shelley, Goethe, William Blake, Hugo, Viollet-le-Duc, Owen Jones; later Whitman, and others.

[3] *Autobiography*, p. 26.

[4] *Autobiography*, p. 478.

[5] The code required a diameter of 90 cm, the shaft's diameter was 22 cm; it was 7.30 m high, whereas the regulations would only allow 182 cm for a diameter of 22 cm. In tests, the elegant shaft could support a load of 60 tons – only 12 were required. *Autobiography*, p. 481.

[6] Lecture given at the Arts and Crafts Society and published in the annual catalogue of the Chicago Architectural Club.

ORNAMENT AND MACHINE

Imperial Hotel, Tokyo.
Viewed from the north
garden, the 'bridge'
linking the bedroom
wings to the main
entrance lobby.

founders of the Arts and Crafts movement – William Morris, who regarded the machine as the arch-enemy,[1] and Ruskin, with his idea of industry as negativity. Wright hoped to be able to 'Make our machine power really beneficent'[2] and at the founding of the Taliesin Fellowship he affirmed the same objective as the Bauhaus: 'integrate art and industry'.[3] He showed great originality even compared to Sullivan who, he said, 'seemed unaware of the machine as a direct element in architecture'.[4] Other Americans such as Baron Jenney were closely interested in the use of machines in building – and why not in architecture? – as one of Wright's favourite authors, Violet-le-Duc had proposed.[5] Concerning the Glass Skyscraper of 1924, Wright went so far as to write 'The aim in this fabrication employing the cantilever system of construction was to achieve absolute scientific utility by means of the Machine. To accomplish – first of all – a true standardization which would not only serve as the basis for keeping the life of the building true as architecture but enable me to project the whole, as an expression of a valuable principle involved, into a genuine living architecture of the present.'[6]

In the Prairie houses, the machine made possible a new creative effect of 'organic simplicity'.[7] It offered a new kind of finish, in more flowing lines, for the joinery and panelling.[8] To this must also be added the repetition which became a principle of the design as a whole and of the decor, and which could be considered as the authentic expression of the age of the machine. In the Prairie house, 'this great simple thing', there were two aspects to the design: on the one hand there was 'a yearning for simplicity',[9] the recognition of the 'definitively decorative value of the plain surface',[10] 'the gospel of the elimination of insignificant preached by the print';[11] and on the other hand was the sculptural effect peculiar to the intelligent use of the machine. The machine does not suppress ornament, it transforms it: the windows or grilles are treated significantly through the mechanical *repetition* of an often very simple motif. A square, for example, becomes a series of squares ordered in accordance with a shape which is itself geometrical, as for example in the clusters of identical little cubes which adorn the pilasters of the Unity Temple or the friezes of the Barnsdall house. Wright explored different methods of mechanical proliferation of interior decoration. Entire wall surfaces in the Midway Gardens were covered in repetitive machine-made decoration. The major work of the Mrs Cheney period – along with the first Taliesin – the Midway Gardens restaurant-dance hall complex (1913–14), which is now gone, marked a turn towards a decorated mineral finish which culminated in the textured concrete blocks used in California and Arizona (1921–29). At the end of the 1920s, in the

[1] William Morris, *Collected Works* 1915, vol. 22, pp. 335–6.

[2] *Autobiography*, p. 336.

[3] 'We believe that a rational attempt to integrate Art and Industry should coordinate both with the everyday life we live here in America'. *Autobiography*, p. 390.

[4] *Autobiography*, p. 107.

p. 71

[5] 'I believed the *Raisonée* was the only really sensible book on architecture in the world… This book was enough to keep, in spite of architects, one's faith alive in architecture.' *Autobiography*, p. 75.

[6] *Autobiography*, p. 259.

[7] *Autobiography*, p. 144.

[8] 'Machine-resources of this period were so little understood that extensive drawings had to be made merely to show the mill-man what to leave off.' *Autobiography*, p. 143.

[9] *Autobiography*, p. 139.

[10] *Autobiography*, p. 110 (concerning the Charnley house).

[11] *Autobiography*, p. 205.

Midway Gardens,
Chicago, 1913–14. Top:
the interior terraces.
Bottom: the central mass
seen from the street.

development of a Modernist modernity, Wright used repetition, in particular in the treatment of the window joinery, repetition of vertical lines in the Elisabeth Noble Apartment and the Lloyd-Jones house (both from 1929), repetition of horizontals in the 'house on the Mesa' (1931), and again in 1948 for the Clinton Walker house. Even during his brief Modernist phase,[1] Wright stood out from other innovators of modern architecture by rejecting maximum austerity. 'Five lines where three are enough is always stupidity. Nine pounds where three are sufficient is obesity. But to eliminate expressive words in speaking or writing – words that intensify or vivify meaning is not simplicity. In architecture, expressive changes of surface, emphasis of line and especially textures of material or imaginative pattern, may go to make facts more eloquent – forms more significant.'[2] The designs for the Johnson Wax Company buildings were explicitly governed by the principle of simplicity,[3] whereas for the moderately-priced house, Wright first of all advocated doing away with pitched roofs, the garage, the guttering, the basement, the visible radiators, the furniture, the plaster finish and the paintwork – and then proposed the industrial prefabrication of lightweight insulating walls, and of door and window frames. The Usonian house was 'a unique house, adapted to prefabrication' for which 'it is necessary to use work in the mill to good advantage, necessary to eliminate as far as possible field labor which is always expensive.'[4]

IN THE NATURE OF MATERIALS

As for the wood partitions, Wright proposed fabricating them in a single operation, with three thicknesses of board screwed together. The joints between the external boards were covered by laths which gave a pattern to the wall and themselves constituted the 'decor', which was not superimposed but intrinsic to the nature of the partition wall. The material and construction thus remained visible, incorporated in the visual effect.[5] Instead of plastering and painting the wood, Wright advocated 'a coating of clear resinous oil',[6] or a colouring which highlighted the material without detracting from its intrinsic qualities. Wright believed on several occasions that he had discovered the 'nature' of concrete. Before leading him to textured concrete blocks and wide cantilevered overhangs, the search for an architectural form particular to this essentially plastic, mouldable material led him to build those smooth, sometimes battered masses,[7] as exemplified by the Unity Temple, the Yamamura House (1918) and the Barnsdall 'Hollyhock' house. The 'capitals' of the Unity Temple, the first manifestation of the idea of concrete as 'able to receive the imprint of the imagination',[8] were transformed into a symbol which

[1] From 1938 onwards, there was a partial return to decorative ornamentation, as shown in the clerestories of the Pope-Leighey and Schwartz houses of 1939, for example, or in the Manson house of 1940, as well as the decoupages and the varied textures of the buildings of the Southern Florida College (from 1939 onwards), etc.

[2] *Autobiography*, p. 144.

[3] 'Owing to a high ideal of simplicity, this building was bound to be an exacting piece of work ... to preserve the great simplicity, I made some 132 trips by motor car from Taliesin to Racine (a distance of 165 miles).' *Autobiography*, p. 469–70.

[4] *Autobiography*, p. 490.

[5] *Autobiography*, p. 336.

[6] *Autobiography*, p. 491.

[7] 'Batter' is an architectural term referring to the inclination of a wall.

[8] *Autobiography*, p. 156.

was independent of structural function in the corncobs of the Universal Portland Cement Company Pavilion built in Madison Square Garden in 1910, and the stylized, mechanized hollyhock motif in the Barnsdall house.

THE METAPHOR

A significant advance was made towards 1921 with the Maya houses, which embodied the two ideas of the shell: the monolithic building and the 'textile block'. The Millard house in Pasadena (1921–23), 'La Miniatura', is the very model of the shell made of shells. Built without foundations, placed on the ground like a gigantic monolith, the house would fall flat on its face if the ground subsided, like those Second World War bunkers on the French Atlantic beaches that time has overturned. The walls of La Miniatura were made of two leaves linked by steel ties each made of concrete blocks which were themselves knit together by steel ties. The walls were thus thin reinforced slabs, textured by motifs moulded into the blocks in the manufacturing process. The rich incrustation of shells made the mineral wall of La Miniatura undulate slightly, while the inclusion of glass blocks among the concrete blocks animated the interior walls with a play of light that had never before been achieved or imagined. This rich ornamentation became 'a legitimate feature of construction'.[1]

[1] *Autobiography*, p. 239.

In complete contrast to the contemporary 'analytical' work of Le Corbusier, who was dissociating as far as possible the various functions of the architectural elements, Wright's Los Angeles houses were a synthesis of the manipulation of space not only with the structure of the building, but with the most elaborate textural ornament. The Maya houses were particularly representative of the Wrightian doctrine of unity, a fundamental unity at the conceptual root of the design. Summarizing his ideas on the use of the concrete block, 'the cheapest (and ugliest) thing in the building', Wright recapitulated the qualities of concrete: 'Concrete was the inert mass and would take compression . . . a plastic material – susceptible to the impress of imagination . . . I saw a kind of weaving coming out of it. Why not weave a kind of building? Then I saw the shell. Shells with steel inlaid in them.'[2] So his imagination was carried along on a wave of poetry: one image followed another, and little by little a design emerged that was both scientific and artistic.

[2] *Autobiography*, p. 235.

For the structure of the Imperial Hotel, several metaphors succeed one another: 'the two hands thrust together palms inward, fingers interlocking', then, a little further on, 'the floors [supported] as a waiter carries his tray on upraised arm and fingers at the center – balancing the load.'[3]

[3] *Autobiography*, p. 206.

For the Glass Skyscraper the metaphor is even more

anthropomorphic[1] but in general it is above all else organic. The Ocatillo Desert Camp brought together four metaphors: the dragonfly (since it was 'ephemeral'), the sailing boat (being hung with white canvas), the talus (from the geometry of the cabins and of the overall plan) and, most important, the ocatillo flower (whence its name) for the geometry and the colour: 'we will paint the canvas one-two triangles in the eccentric gables scarlet. The one-two triangles of the ocatillo bloom itself are scarlet.'[2] Wright loved Arizona, where he found a stimulating landscape and also a rich reserve of metaphors which were both organic and structural. 'The great nature-masonry ... is inspiration. A pattern of what appropriate Arizona architecture might well lie there hidden in the Sahuaro. The Sahuaro, perfect example of reinforced building construction ... in these desert constructions he (architect or engineer) may not only see the reinforcing-rod scientifically employed as in the flesh of the Sahuaro but he may see the perfect lattice or the reed and welded tubular construction in the stalk of the cholla, or staghorn, and see it too in the cellular build-up of the water-barrel, Bignana. Even the flesh of the prickly pear is worth studying for scientific structure.'[3]

'Conceive now that an entire building might grow up out of conditions as a plant grows up out of soil and yet be free to be itself, to "live its own life according to Man's Nature". Dignified as a tree in the midst of nature but a child of the spirit of man. I now propose an ideal for the architecture of the machine age, for the ideal American building. Let it grow up in that image. The tree. But I do not mean to suggest the imitation of the tree.'[4] Indeed there is no analogical relationship at all between the metaphor and the architectural element concerned, no literal 'interpretation'. The Ocatillo Camp in no way resembles a swarm of gigantic butterflies, but that is how Wright 'saw' the cabins 'conforming gracefully to the crown of the outcropping of black splintered rock gently uprising from the desert floor.'[5] However, this metaphor was the idea behind the design of the temporary habitat in the desert, as Wright explains in the pages which follow our quotation. No butterfly symbolism, and yet there was something, a trace, an echo behind the sheer architecturality of Wright's work. As with San Marcos-in-the-Desert and its sahuaro,[6] the metaphor introduced a remoteness – the Ocatillo Camp was not a representation of a colony of butterflies but a re-creation. To draw a butterfly is to make a representation of it, but through the process of language the metaphor becomes a shape, represents an ideogram, strictly abstract, architectural, in which the features of the butterfly are present, but scattered, like an abstruse allusion – which is the very definition of metaphor.

[1] 'The construction balanced as the body on the legs, the walls hanging at the arms from the shoulders, and the whole heavy only where weight ensures stability.' *Autobiography*, p. 258.

[2] *Autobiography*, p. 311.

[3] *Autobiography*, p. 310.

[4] *Autobiography*, p. 147.

[5] *Autobiography*, p. 310.

[6] 'The building was to grow up out of the desert by way of desert materials. The block system naturally as the Sahuaro grew up. The Sahuaro should be the motif that inspired its style and the details.' *Autobiography*, p. 307. But there is nothing cactus-like about San Marcos.

Below: the internal
courtyard of the
Barnsdall 'Hollyhock'
house, Los Angeles,
1917–21.

Opposite: main
façade, over the
garden, of the Millard
house, 'La Miniatura',
Pasadena, California,
1921–3.

Taliesin West,
Scottsdale, Arizona,
1938. Dotted lines and
textured planes.

[1] *Autobiography*, pp. 146–7.

[2] In the most well-known presentation perspective, the organic curve is replaced by geometrical belt courses like corbelling stones.

[3] 'Always the desire to get some system of building construction as a basis for architecture was my objective – my hope. There never was, there is no architecture otherwise, I believe.' *Autobiography*, p. 234.

[4] 'The main feature of construction was the simple repetition of slender hollow monolithic dendriform shafts or stems – the stems standing tip-toe in small brass shoes bedded at the floor level.' *Autobiography*, p. 472.

[5] The Williams and Moore houses (1895), the Hickox house (1900), the great banqueting hall of the Imperial Hotel, the cabins on Lake Tahoe (1922), the Gladney house (1925), the Camping Water Gardens of Dr Chandler (1927–8), the Rosenwald Foundation (1929), the First Unitarian Church (1949), the roof in corrugated steel on the pavilion in New York (1953), the Boomer house (1953), and the Hoffman house (1955), etc.

[6] Jacobs I (1937), Rosenbaum (1939), Baird and Pope-Leighey (1940)

For his structural designs Wright would borrow the fluid and supple adaptability of plant life, where stem and leaf join together in a gracious play of curves. 'Now why not let walls, ceilings, and floors be SEEN as mutual component parts of each other, their surfaces flowing into each other? To get continuity in the whole, eliminating all constructed features...'.[1] This structural principle integrates the vertical (post) and the horizontal (beam and slab) into a single structural organism, as opposed to the structure whose components are separate and distinctly assembled. But this is mostly a matter of structural principle, not of morphology: even the large cantilevers were sometimes jointed (for example in the Sturges house, and the Johnson Wax Building shafts), and were rarely fluid as in Fallingwater (as built).[2] In La Miniatura the masses were articulated although the building was designed as a structural entity of absolute continuity. The morphology of the building only sometimes followed the structural principle, although this is so basic to architecture.[3]

Sometimes the structure was treated with refinement,[4] but Wright was never concerned to 'display' the construction in the European way. In some cases even the main beams were concealed, and barely hinted at by the decoration – so that even the trained eye might find the structure difficult to follow – for example the huge metal beams that facilitate the enfilades of windows and spectacular overhangs of the Prairie houses.

In the Maya houses the system of prefabrication became the decorative motif, the semantic and the technical being held in balance; but in Taliesin West the beams became a sort of symbolic gesture. There, the semantic is dominant; it absorbs the functional, and transforms it into writing, into a symbol. The canopy which links Fallingwater to the guest annexe, and numerous other examples of folded forms[5] – as in the Origami aesthetic that seems to emerge in some of the fragile Usonian houses[6] – are also symbolic.

GENIUS LOCI

Throughout the autobiography, as in his other writing, Wright takes an obvious pleasure in pastoral description, in particular in the various visions which little by little built up the image of Taliesin. His writing reveals an exceptional sensitivity to the natural environment and through this to the 'visionary', to physical matter and how it is experienced. Seldom has an architect transcended the technical qualities of his materials, as Wright does, by attaching to them the

Top: the covered
'promenade' between
the Kaufmann house
and the guest house,
Bear Run, Pennsylvania,
1939. Bottom: the
Unitarian Church at
Madison, Wisconsin,
1949–50. The main hall
seen from the street.

[1] 'Clusters of pod-topped weeds woven of bronze here and there sprinkling the spotless expanse of white. Dark sprays of slender metallic straight lines, tipped with quivering dots. Pattern to the eye of the sun, as the sun spread delicate network of more pattern in blue shadows on the white beneath.' *Autobiography*, p. 3.

[2] 'The field is brown, with that unctuous purple-brown of freshly turned earth . . . A faint green tinge covers the brown field. The wood is flecked with green and touched with delicate pink. The bobwhite have been calling the Spring for two weeks past.' *Autobiography*, p. 61.

[3] *Autobiography*, p. 173.

[4] *Autobiography*, p. 170.

[5] 'It is fun to plan meals with our young people. For instance: as to what meat we shall use this week – shall we butcher the calf or the pig or the goat-kid, geese or chickens? We would wander together through our old cook books, some of them fifty years old: American, Russian, Yugoslav, Polish: of all nations really, and find new delicacies, always learning new exciting ways and always succeeding in getting interesting meals prepared.' *Autobiography*, p. 426.

[6] *Autobiography*, p. 169.

[7] *Autobiography*, p. 173.

[8] *Autobiography*, p. 399.

[9] *Autobiography*, p. 173.

[10] An effect particularly seen in the Imperial Hotel, for example in the cantilevered slabs on the exterior or in the towers of screen walls which articulate the main entrance hall.

vision of a painter, as sensitive to line[1] as to colour[2] – a vision which is overwhelmed in its turn by the presence of physical sensation and emotional experience.[3] The architect's drawing and the photograph do not convey the sounds, the smells, the feel of the materials, the experience of ascending and descending, in the sunshine, in the shelter from the rain, in a high wind, or on gravel paths crunching underfoot. Wright insisted on locating ponds in each open courtyard of Taliesin[4] or decorative fountains in luxury houses – the Dana house (1902), the Price Senior house (1954), where the water modifies the artificial ambience of the architecture not only by imparting humidity but by its scent, its murmur, its shifting reflections. This sensitivity of Wright's is conveyed in many sensuous passages in the autobiography,[5] from the vision of Taliesin: 'I saw the hill-crown back of the house as one mass of apple trees in bloom, drifting down the Valley . . . I remembered the rich odor of blackcurrants . . .'[6] to its realization: 'In spring, the perfume of the blossoms came full through the windows, the birds singing there the while, from sunrise to sunset – all but the several white months of winter.'[7]

In the spirit of traditional Japanese art Wright did not concentrate on the summer and the sun, but valued equally half-light, the mist and the snow. At the founding of the Taliesin Fellowship, he designed two significant letter-heads: one represented Hillside under snow, and the other Taliesin under snow.[8] The architect would modify his plans in response to the weather to obtain a poetic effect. Thus at Taliesin: 'I wanted a home where icicles by invitation might beautify the eaves. So there were no gutters. And when the snow piled deep on the roofs and lay drifted in the courts, icicles came to hang staccato from the eaves. Prismatic crystal pendants sometimes six feet long, glittered between the landscape and the eyes inside. Taliesin in winter was a frosted palace roofed and walled with snow, hung with iridescent fringes . . .'[9]

Light is a natural phenomenon that alters continually, and Wright used it more or less as the Zen Master of the Way of the Gardens used the mountain or the fountain water reverberating in the bamboos. The play of light and shade is often thought of as a sculptural thing, but in Wright's case – whether in an isolated sunbeam or a passing shower of light through a perforated screen[10] – the movement of the light produces not sculpture, but a kind of writing. What it writes is not shadow, but a living sign across a pool of shadow, a sublime sign without a message.

The snow-covered
gable of the Springfield
house, Illinois, 1900–2.

THE IDEAL
WIFE

[1] *Autobiography*, p. 478.
Concerning the Johnson
house 'Wingspread'.

[2] *Autobiography*, p. 169.

Sometimes when the site was unattractive it was transformed by the
design: the building gave significance to the landscape and 'the site
seems to come alive'.[1] The purpose of each design was to find the
ideal 'spouse' for the site. At Taliesin, Wright had at his disposal a hill;
hill and house had to live together 'each the happier for the other . . .
Yes, there was a house that this hill might marry and live happily with
ever after. I fully intended to find it; I even saw for myself what it might
be like.'[2] Taliesin had to belong to the hill, be *of* and not *on* the hill;
hence its name, which in Welsh means 'shining brow'; it had to spring

from the soil, from the ground of Wright's ancestry and rural child-
hood, just as 'a plant grows and develops from the ground'.[1] The place
– and particularly its soil – would develop from a metonymy into a
metaphor of the design: a metaphor which expanded to embrace all
the elements of the site, from the silhouette of the house (the view of
the hills) to the solidity of the stone walls (the 'quarry as a model') and
the wood (the trees below), as if Wright was trying to make a synthesis
of his roots. 'There was a stone quarry on another hill a mile away, where
the yellow sand-limestone uncovered lay in strata like outcropping

[1] *Autobiography*, p. 170.

The living room of
Taliesin I, 1911.
Furniture designed by
Wright.

ledges in the façades of the hills. The look of it was what I wanted for such masses as would raise from these native slopes . . . Taliesin was to be an abstract combination of stone and wood as they naturally met in the aspect of the hills around about. The lines of the hills were the lines of the roofs, the slopes of the hills their slopes, the plastered surface of the light wood-walls, set back into shade beneath broad eaves, were like the flat stretches of sand in the river below, and the same in color, for that is where the material that covered them came from. The finished wood outside was the color of gray tree trunks in violet light. The shingles of the roof surfaces were left to weather silver-gray like the tree branches spreading below them.'[1] Does the stone wall pretend to be 'natural'? Its material is certainly 'raw'; the walls of Taliesin came straight from the nearby quarry. It was what linguists call a 'seme', a romantic seme but nevertheless a seme, significant, symbolic, whose power as a motif Wright himself surely felt since he made it the principal ornament of Taliesin. But this 'seme' was not mythological: it did not pretend to be 'natural', in the obvious sense; it did not follow the common rule. The walls of Taliesin are not the walls of any Wisconsin farm. On the contrary, it signalled Wright's passage, it was a signature, it was unique.

Previous to Taliesin, Wright's stonework tended to be square-cut blocks, with the roughened surfaces of which Richardson was so fond; from Taliesin onwards it was no longer the design which dictated the material, but the site. In forest areas, the Taliesin motif was frequently repeated, with its long irregular rectangles not always on the level.[2] In the canyons of Los Angeles,[3] as in the deserts of Arizona,[4] the building would rise from its terrain. In San Marcos, Ocatillo and later Taliesin West, the building became, as at Taliesin, an 'analogue' of the site, reflecting the terrain and with the same spread of the metaphor into any available metonymy. The building assumed the colour of a flower of the desert or that of the 'dry rose as the color to match the light on the desert floor';[5] its structure was inspired by the cells of a cactus, it borrowed the sails from the boats on the Mesa river, and its triangular profile mirrored the outline of the mountain ranges.[6] Even the straight line takes the imprint of its surroundings. 'The straight line and flat plane must come here – of all places – but they should become the dotted line, the broad, low, extended plane textured because in all this astounding desert there is not one hard undotted line to be seen. Now, observe if you will that every horizontal line in San Marcos in the Desert is a dotted line. The entire building is in pattern an abstraction of mountain region and cactus life . . . The whole building is made more cactus than any cactus can be in itself . . . Arizona desert itself was architectural inspiration to me and

[1] *Autobiography*, p. 171.

[2] 'Country masons laid all the stone with the stone-quarry for a pattern and the architect for a teacher. The masons learned to lay the walls in the long, thin, flat ledges natural to the quarry.' *Autobiography*, p. 171.

[3] 'The best thing I had . . . to begin with, was something that belonged to the ground on which it stood.' *Autobiography*, p. 241, concerning La Miniatura which, in the middle of its eucalyptus valley, did indeed resemble a giant brightly-coloured fungus.

[4] *Autobiography*, p. 305.

[5] *Autobiography*, p. 311.

[6] *Autobiography*, p. 310.

because it was actually the architect's workshop in this endeavour, the feeling of the whole building in all its parts now designedly belongs to the terrain. This is what I mean by indigenous architecture.'[1] In Taliesin West, Wright created this ideal not with textile block patterns but with a third and final type of stonework: 'desert concrete', rough, cyclopean like the surrounding landscape, cast with a strong batter like scree on a hillside, a concrete at once romantic, futuristic and expressive. In 1953, in Phoenix, Wright built side by side the Boomer house in desert concrete and the Adelman house in textile blocks, each one in harmony, in its own way, with the Arizona desert.

[1] *Autobiography*, p. 314 (concerning San Marcos-in-the-Desert).

TOWN AND COUNTRY

Three American landscapes took part in Wright's architectural output: humid (Wisconsin), dry (California), desert (Arizona).[2] All his writings disparage the town: a place of artificial society, of degradation, of dishonourable behaviour, it is in opposition to the country, where one can return to one's roots, and one's senses. The myth of nature drew him out to a countryside which had almost disappeared even in the 1920s. By this time big business capitalism was invading the country-side and attempting to make it profitable through intensive cultivation, based on the model of industry. The process is excellently typified in a picture from a school book: an imposing combine harvester operated

[2] The pre-1910 residential areas of Chicago, Oak Park and River Forest, were in some ways substitutes for the countryside.

Taliesin West, Scottsdale, Arizona, 1938. Page 84, top: overall view with the studio on the left. Bottom: fountain in a back court. Page 85, top: the studio gable; in the foreground, the 'treasure'; on the left, the pergola (see p. 101). Bottom: living area (see p. 99, top); typical 'desert concrete' wall in the foreground. Page 86: back wall. Page 87, top: the first Jacobs house, Westmoreland, Wisconsin, 1936–7, often acclaimed by Wright as the first Usonian house. Bottom: Boomer house, Phoenix, Arizona, 1953. The entrance with porch; on the right the wall protecting the enclosed garden.

by a single man, devouring a sea of wheat which stretches out to the horizon. The countryside to which Wright aspired was the near desert of the pioneers, and it was only to be expected that after the secluded countryside of Wisconsin, 56 kilometres outside Madison and seven kilometres from the nearest village, he would eventually move to a real desert, in Arizona.[1]

Chicago had come as a great shock to the young Wright: 'so cold, black, blue-white and wet. The horrid blue-white glare of arc-lights was over everything. Shivering. Hungry.'[2] The coldness of the city dwellers, the brutal dissonance, the bewildering names, the languages of the new Babylon, nothing friendly or attractive. 'Chicago . . . cross-currents of horses, trucks, street cars grinding on hard rails mingling with streams of human beings in seeming confusion and clamor . . . Dreary-dim-smoked. Smoked dim and smoking. Terrible, this grinding and piling up of blind forces. If there was logic here who could grasp it?'[3]

The answer lay in architecture, so long wished for and dreamed of, and for so long impossible to find in the general mediocrity of the immense city. Wright seemed to treasure pleasant memories of Madison, the small town he had just left, but in fact it was its provincial quality which spoke to him: 'Madison is a beautiful city. From near or far away the white dome of the State Capitol on a low spreading hill shone white in the sun between two blue lakes, Mendota and Monona. Two more, smaller, not so blue, Wingra and Waubesa, were flung one side for good measure.'[4] Like many 'modernists' from the first half of the century, Wright found nothing worth conserving in the big city. He was an advocate of the countryside and in his proposals for urban development the town ultimately dissolved into a countryside punctuated by individual or collective dwellings, as in Broadacre City. 'As agrarian as it was urban',[5] this was a rather over-simplistic attempt to fix in one huge idea Wright's American ideal, this Usony anchored in an enthusiastic faith since his youth, since 1893 when he turned down the offer of going to Paris to follow the teaching of old Europe.

[1] 'The Big City is no longer a place for more than the exterior applications of some cliche or sterile formula, where life is concerned. Therefore the Taliesin Fellowship chooses to live and work in the country.' *Autobiography*, p. 391.

[2] *Autobiography*, p. 63.

[3] *Autobiography*, pp. 65–6.

[4] *Autobiography*, p. 30.

[5] *Autobiography*, p. 500.

Top: dining corner in the Willey house, Minneapolis, 1934. Bottom: Pauson house, Phoenix, Arizona, 1939–40 (destroyed by a fire in 1942).

Mobilis in mobile

Top: the Pew house in the snow, Shorewood Hills, Wisconsin, 1940. Bottom: the Pew house and the Mendota lake.

The Pew house, built in 1940 by Taliesin apprentices, is one of the classic buildings of the Usonian period. An inexpensive project, it was built exclusively from stone and cypress, both inside and out. A dark porch opens directly into the living room, with a superb view over Lake Mendota through a wall of eight French windows, the last two of which, placed at right angles, fold back to open up the panorama. In the foreground the large terrace stretching out like the deck of a ship, further emphasizes the horizontal of the lake. Inside, the living room stretches out on both sides of a large fireplace decorated with a rock as a lintel, set off by a corresponding inset in the ceiling. Behind the fireplace the dining area opens onto the kitchen. All these areas, each with its own character, are positioned in such a way as to emphasize the straight lines and the diagonals, and to accentuate the width of the available space.

The first floor is slightly offset in relation to the ground floor. The roof of the living area provides a terrace which is accessed from the landing. Each of the three bedrooms is lit by a corner window shaded by a small canopy. The living room and terrace at the front of the house rest on a massive stone pier, as the ground falls away to the water below. Raised terraces reinforce the nautical image of the interior, but this is not the white liner of Le Corbusier or Art deco, so much as a skiff or sailing boat with its warm-toned woodwork. While the large platform, the high terrace and the internal ambience give this building a modern boat-like (or bridge-like) appearance, the fireplace and the piers of rustic masonry associate it once more with an aesthetic of earth and cave. It floats among the trees – the metaphor belongs to H.R. Hitchcock[1] – but it is also part of the hillside, whose movement it follows with its own profile. The house has a dual nature – it is both dynamic and domestic – and it has a special charm.

[1] Hitchcock, p. 97.

THE BRIDGE

[2] Other projects joined around a bridge: Wolf Lake (1895), Doheny (1921), Lake Tahoe (1922), Kaufmann (1936).

[3] Hillside Home School (1902), Imperial Hotel (1916), Johnson Wax Company (1936), Adelman laundry (1946) and the following houses: Glasner (1905), Gerts (1906), Coonley (1908), Schroeder (1912), Barnsdall (1920), Millard (1922), Ennis (1923), Pauson (1940), Jacobs II (1943) and D. Wright (1950).

The archetype of the bridge is also employed in some very beautiful plans for houses built around a bridge: the most striking is without doubt the design for S. Booth (1911), for whom Wright actually designed a bridge at Ravine Bluffs in 1915.[2] Other houses simply used the idea of the bridge or the tunnel.[3] At the end of his life Wright would amuse himself by designing big bridges for Pittsburgh (1947), for Wisconsin (1947), for the San Francisco Bay (1949), not forgetting the inhabited bridge which is the Marin County Civic Center (1957). He loved the principles of ballast, counterweight, cantilever, suspension . . . which were developed during the Industrial Revolution for the construction of large-span bridges.

With the cantilevers that metal construction made possible, Wright was able to design his two most spectacular buildings, the Robie

house in 1908 and Fallingwater in 1936. Metal also facilitated the structural design of the Imperial Hotel: thanks to the systematic use of the double cantilever in equilibrium on central supports, the hotel floated on the silt like 'a battleship floats on salt water'.[1]

[1] *Autobiography*, p. 214.

On the west face of Taliesin, the house extends over the void. The Sturges house (1939), the Oboler house ('Eagle Feather', 1940), and the Morris house (first plan, 1946) were composed entirely of overhangs jutting out in front like bridges towards infinity. At the prow of these ships one leans out towards the horizon; the countryside becomes a panorama; it seems to yield itself up but at the same time it slips away, inaccessible. Thus theatrically keeping the world at arm's length, often perched in the middle of a clearing, they were spectacular, dramatic eyries. The most superb example of this is certainly the Sturges house, built at Brentwood in 1939; the photographs always show the house in the midst of luxuriant Californian vegetation, with its magnificent balcony secured to the gigantic chimney which anchors it to the hill. But below this proud 'rock' lies not a chaos of rubble shattered by the storm, but about 20 small detached houses, each more mediocre than the other. We are not in a jungle (at least only in the social sense), this is an urban milieu, quite devoid of architectural distinction. With the 'development' of this part of the canyon, any flight of lyricism now seems only a touching fantasy, at once tragic and pathetic. But still there is power which shines from this astonishing architectural feat – a tiny house of barely three rooms.

THE CAVE

If the image of the leaping bridge pervades all Wright's work, its opposite, the tunnel, is also present. Wright did not produce any literally subterranean architecture, but he did build several houses which were half-buried. When presenting the prototype for the Cooperative Homesteads of 1942, and the Keyes house of 1952, Wright quoted only the practical and economic advantages of building underground, the savings on external walls and insulation.[2] A long double-pitched roof, hollow inside, and a wide slab surmount like a peaked cap, large masonry piers and a narrow window that almost encircles the house. This roof, edged by earth banks, spans a central passage which serves as a car port and entrance porch: big doors open directly into the living room in which are several 'corners': kitchen, dining area, fireplace.

[2] FLW, *The natural house*, p. 148.

Aside from the practicality, the imagery of the cavern underlay all Wright's work. All his public buildings, for example, were caves metamorphosed by the art of construction, as if humanity wished to be in sympathy with its troglodytic roots.[3] The metaphor frequently

[3] An imagination drawn towards phylogenesis would then refer back elastic metal, the bridge, the boat and the promontory to these other beginnings of human habitation as seen in the lakeside pile dwellings.

appears in the writing of critics. Taking the abstract example of the
Unity Temple of 1906, Marcello Angrisani speaks of the circulation of
the 'almost "cavernous" darkness of the corridors to the diffused light
of the auditorium'.[1] Vincent Scully, whose cultural parallels are
sometimes out of place, sees the megalithic cave in the circular
houses from the forties; in Fallingwater, 'the interior cavern is well and
truly sealed in the rock and opens on to the pavilion which dominates
the water'.[2]

[1] M. Angrisani, in the
catalogue *FLW drawings*,
Centro Di.

[2] V. Scully, *FLW*, p. 26.

MASSES

Always, great masses of stone give the building a feeling of
permanence. The mass is sometimes functional, as in the buried
houses, or when it provides ballast for a big overhang, but its
significance, like that of the fireplace, is above all symbolic. The
mineral mass *par excellence* – the fireplace – is never a mere piece
of heating equipment, and it is not a trivial feature: it is a 'veritable
hearth'. Thinking of his early houses, Wright recalled his desire for
wide chimney-breasts, generous and low chimneys: 'It comforted me
to see the fire burning deep in the solid masonry of the house itself'.[1]
From 1899/1902, the fireplace was the core of the house and the fire
which brightened this centre became the living symbol of the very
life which the house sheltered. The geometry of this central mass was
often strikingly and starkly modernistic. It was the centre of the cross-
shape of the Prairie house, from which the building radiated. The
Willitts house of 1902, the first to offer the fully cruciform arrangement

[1] *Autobiography*, p. 141.

Top: the banqueting
hall in the Imperial
Hotel, Tokyo, 1914–21.
Bottom: the playroom
(1893) in the Wright
house at Oak Park.

[1] See the Dana, Martin,
Coonley, Little and
Barnsdall houses, as well as
Taliesin, Taliesin West and
some other large plans
which were not built such
as the McCormick and
Booth houses.

[2] Lowell Walter house
(1945) and Edwards house
(1949).

[3] There were, in Wright's
opinion, some true domes –
Saint-Sophia – which
respected real forces; but
there were also false ones,
which were contrived, by
means of some stratagem,
such as iron chains, and
looked unnatural: the
sculptor's dome, the
'unnatural masonry of Saint
Peter's in Rome'.
Autobiography, p. 335.

characteristic of the 'Prairie' style, made another use of the masonry mass, arranging it in a peripheral 'crown' of low walls which anchored the house to its garden and which could be transformed, in the case of a large residence, into a series of galleries and annexes.[1] The Usonian houses presented a variant of this peripheral crown device: from 1930 onwards there was no further call for big houses, and architectural organization compensated for the loss of sheer substance. Firstly, this was achieved by means of the emphasis on minerality: the walls were often made of the rough masonry inspired by the stone of the Taliesin region, which Wright preferred to smooth (and therefore more abstract) materials such as brick, cement or plaster, the usual materials of the Prairie houses. Secondly, he used the form of centralized organization, in which the piers were more numerous and sometimes formed a full or partial ring. The centre could be occupied in various ways: by an aquatic sunken garden in the second (half-underground) Jacobs house (1943); by a void as in the (elevated) D. Wright house (1950); by the habitable core of the house, as in the Friedman house (1950), whose focal point was duplicated to accentuate even further the effect of the mass. The hollow crown is obviously found again in Wright's massive building *par excellence*, the Guggenheim Museum.

While many Usonian houses were made of regular rectangular, partially offset constructions,[2] some are disparate, more or less crystalline clusters of angular blocks. Although this type of plan is rare for a house, intersecting volumes are common in public buildings. Blocks might be juxtaposed on a horizontal axis or else stacked up on a vertical axis, an axis of symmetry, which arrangement imparts an impression of strength and power. The Pfeiffer chapel (1940) at Florida Southern College combined the two techniques: the plan was a rectangle and a hexagon overlaid, and in the 'lantern' over the pulpit solid forms fitted together with suspended trellises designed for climbing plants. The pulpit of the First Unitarian Church in Madison (1950) was a conglomeration of geometric rocks jammed in a crevice; as in the Pfeiffer chapel, this was emphasized by the lighting. In both buildings the main source of natural light was obstructed by metaphorical rocks whose arrangement constituted true caves, in vault or dome form. For Wright, the vault was the optimum interior cavity, it should not be transformed into a dome, like a 'new Saint Peter's'.[3] He used not spherical domes, but tunnel vaults, horizontal hemicylinders beneath pitched roofs. The large playroom which was added in 1895 to the Oak Park house, and the main rooms of the first large Prairie house (Dana, 1903) well illustrated this form of the cave. In most of the houses of this period the living room was ceilinged by

Opposite: mezzanine gallery between the main office of the Johnson Wax Company and the entrance lobby. Page 98: interior of the 'Wigwam' in the Johnson house, 'Wingspread', Wisconsin, 1937.

Page 99: top, interior ambience in Taliesin West, 1938; bottom, living room in the Johnson house. Page 100: main entrance of Taliesin West, 1938. Page 101: rear pergola of Taliesin West, in stained wood.

the rectilinear vault built into the roof void; this device was a factor in the success of the Coonley house (1908) of which Wright was particularly proud. In another major success, the administration building for the Johnson Wax Company (1936), internal spherical vaults covered the reception area of the publicity department and, in a less obvious way, the conference room. Twenty years later, Wright designed domes to be visible on the exterior, on the Greek Orthodox church in Milwaukee (1956) and the Marin County Civic Center, which was built in 1962 after his death. These domes, in contrast to the arrogant affirmation of the classical dome, were more like a slight bulge in the eminent horizontality of the building.

OPENINGS

Most of Wright's buildings ingeniously handled dark passages, bathed in a gentle half-light. Even in the most abstract houses, great areas of walls generated subtle plays of light, and it only required the conjunction of half-darkness and a staircase, a conjunction of which Wright was a past master, to produce the effect of the cave. A number of designs brought the staircase close to the fireplace to form a central mass away from the windows and conducive to back-light or *contre-jour*. Transfused light, which was never harsh, transformed every interior into a revelation of architectural space; Wright loved filtered light and often employed overhead natural lighting, which relativizes natural light.

Concerning the Larkin building (1904) Wright noted that 'the dignified top lighted interior created the effect of one great official family at work'.[1] Zenithal lighting and the use of staircases were fundamental in the design of the Unity Temple (1906): from the entrance foyer of a flight of steps ascends to the main level of the auditorium, which is surrounded by two tiers of balconies. The walls are windowless to the second storey, then behind the upper balcony they become glass screens through which daylight floods, modified by the roof overhang and structural pillars outside. The roof slab is pierced by decorated skylights.

Wright always took great care with his treatment of light, and the form and positioning of windows, with a strong predilection for indirect light and reflections. In the Prairie houses, 'The underside of roof-projections was flat and usually light in color to create a glow of reflected light that softly brightened the upper rooms. Overhangs had double value: shelter and preservation for the walls of the house, as well as this diffusion of reflected light for the upper story through the "light screens" that took the place of the walls and were now often the

[1] *Autobiography*, p. 151.

Below: profile of the Sturges house, Brentwood, California, 1939.

Opposite, top: on the terrace of the Sturges house. Bottom: the Unitarian Church in Madison, Wisconsin, 1950; the glass walls seen from the interior with the awning and the preacher's pulpit.

The large glass wall of
the Unitarian Church in
Madison, Wisconsin,
1950.

windows in long series.'[1] To modulate the stream of light which
poured in through the longitudinal windows, Wright replaced plain
glazing with subtly patterned glass; later, for the Usonian houses, he
added repetitive vertical or horizontal glazing bars, or even, for the
clerestories, boards perforated by decorative designs. To the screens
and partitions of the Prairie period, to the later clefts, breaks and joins
between blocks of masonry, to the circular and low-level openings of
the last works, must be added, to complete this catalogue of the
openings into Wright's cave world, the delicate perforations within the
mineral substance itself, the beautiful textile blocks inset with glass of
the Maya houses of Los Angeles.

[1] *Autobiography*, p. 142.

ATTACHED FORMS

In the Prairie houses, the ceilings which follow the pitch of the roof
sometimes give the impression of a tent.[2] The four Maya houses, made
of stepped terraces in the fashion of the pueblos of New Mexico, were
under construction when Wright designed the Nakoma Country Club
to be built on the site of a former Indian reservation at Wisconsin,
based around five conical tepees. A few of the cabins in the summer
resort on Lake Tahoe (project dated 1922) also illustrate the theme of
the tent. The autobiography reveals an extraordinary contradiction in
Wright's outlook. He designed Dr Chandler's San Marcos-in-the-
Desert, a 'permanent' building to last for 'three hundred years at least';
on the other hand, he maintained that 'we spend too much on making
things last' and built as his own residence in the desert the Ocatillo
Camp, consisting of wood cabins with canvas roofs and windows, an
idea which he used again in Taliesin West. In its diffused light, just as
in its concave geometry, the tent echoes the cave theme; in fact any
contradiction between the most permanent interior and the light and
ephemeral fragility of the tent does not exist in the artistic conception.
The image of the tent reappeared at least twice, first in 1937 in the
Johnson house where, in the wigwam of the large entrance hall, the
profusion of small skylights in the expanse of the roof imparted the
distinctive translucency of the tent. Twenty years later Wright re-used
an old sketch for a cathedral of steel, which he drew in 1925 at the
time of Nakoma, and built the Beth Sholom synagogue (1959), 'a
transparent Sinaï'[3] but also a gigantic tepee of translucent corrugated
plastic, mounted on a concrete boat.
    The enclosed space of the cave could also be transformed into an
eviscerated ruin: the image of the ruin is more dynamic than it might
seem. Like the tent, the ruin is in fact similar to the cave; it is an
exaggerated cave, taken to the extreme, where the yawning gap
which is essential to the idea of the cave becomes the predominant

[2] With regard to Taliesin,
Wright noted that 'the
rooms went up into the roof,
tent-like and were
ribanded overhead with
marking-strips of waxed
soft wood'. *Autobiography*,
p. 173.

[3] Quotation by FLW in B.
Zevi, p. 252.

feature. The ruin is a cave torn apart and flooded by a plethora of
light, and by the weather which has destroyed it and laid it open. It
is liquefied, mineral, organic. The ruin lives on the rain like a plant,
open to the weather and in a permanent process of evolution. Created
by cataclysm and worn away by the incessant work of the elements,
it slowly returns towards the horizontal of mother earth and of the
shore which is, according to tradition, the only thing that remains of
dead empires. A paradoxical mineral since it belongs symbolically to
the organic world, the ruin is perpetually dying; it is a dead thing
which lives and which is teeming with life. Every Wright building, if
it sufficiently encompasses the vision of the cave, plays at being a
mineral charnel house, and this theatricality arouses both revulsion
and fascination. But the taste for the ruin is also a positive affirmation:
in the end, organic life has the upper hand not over the mineral
substance but over the tragedy of destruction. Ivies and lichens,
mosses and ferns, bushes and colourful plants, all these organic
elements which Wright loved to represent on his drawings and which
sometimes inspired his designs, soften the sharp splintering of the
raised and flattened mineral substance, and finally harmony reduces
conflict.

INTERACTION

The two great aesthetics of the bridge and the cave represent two
different worlds but they interacted in Wright's work. This interaction
produces a reconciliation between eternity and the present; it unites
the roughness of the raw material with the smoothness which men
make of all things. Both bridge and cave, modern and romantic,
Wright's buildings inspire pleasure on all counts. Walking through a
Wright building, the sense of confinement and the sensation of cosmic
motion move in a powerful, rhythmic harmony. Unlike designs based
exclusively on a pure and abstract formal logic, it is the movement
which constitutes the unity of Wright's building, an experience which
has to be relived on several occasions before it is fully appreciated.
With regard to the Imperial Hotel, a complex and difficult creation,
Wright spoke of the 'shibui', that special quality which at first we do
not like but which little by little intrigues us until we fall in love with it.[1]

 In all of Wright's buildings, there is hardly one construction which
is, unequivocally, an example of a single aesthetic. The buildings
which make exclusive use of the aesthetic of the bridge are rare: the
first design for V.C. Morris, although modern, was no more than a
stringing together of blocks. Equally, nothing could be less aerial than
the solid opaque matter of the Guggenheim Museum; smooth and
modern, this definitely belongs to the world of metal but its overall

[1] Wendingen, p. 139.

Presentation drawing
for the Smith house,
Piedmont Pines,
California, 1938. Not
built.

Top: fireplace corner in
the D. Wright house,
'How to live in the South-
West', Phoenix, Arizona,
1950. Bottom: Beth
Sholom synagogue,
Elkins Park,
Philadelphia,
Pennsylvania, 1954.

HOUSE FOR MR. AND MRS. E. A. SMITH. PIEDMONT
FRANK LLOYD WRIGHT. ARCH

Top: David Wright house 'How to live in the South-West', Phoenix, Arizona, 1950 (see p. 109). Bottom: the living room of the Friedman house, Pleasantville, New York, 1949–50 (see pp. 121 and 123).

organization around a giant well makes it into the exemplary cave. Perhaps we have an unequivocal building in the Lowell Walter house (1945–49), a sort of prototype for the American house of the fifties with its living room with lots of glass, surmounted by a round-edged slab. The most poetic detail of this building, which was constructed without wood, is certainly the small landing stage below.

It is just as difficult to assign any building unequivocally to the world of the cave. The internal mezzanine, the large expanse of window and its curved overhang link the second Jacobs house, for example, to the modern world, but otherwise it belongs to the world of the cave. Another case is that of the Maya houses, but their basic materials – reinforced concrete textile blocks – were modernist, as were their forms, which were just as much contemporary as they were pre-Columbian: the Ennis and Storrer terraces, the smooth balconies of La Miniatura, the great windows of the Freeman house which so obviously foreshadowed Fallingwater.

Sometimes buildings were no more than combinations of juxtaposed aspects of the cave and the bridge. The Price Senior house (1954) combined massive walls battered like the base of a Japanese fortress, and a great aerial roof, supported by huge flared pillars, creased by the slight projection of each course over the one below. A few dozen centimetres from the roof, these pillars give way to delicate needles decorated with little cubes. The house is organized around an atrium with the grandeur of a neo-classical mansion although it is free from any Graeco-Roman quotations. Also battered but in rusticated masonry (in the Mannerist sense of the term), the walls of the Friedman house (1949) define the building as a circular core which throws out tentacles around it. The squat masses welded to the ground, the chaotic intensity of the interiors, recall Taliesin West, as does its gigantic masses of masonry stuck crookedly into the soil. Everything inside has overtones of 'barbarism': the multicoloured fabrics and rugs, the geometrical furniture, the canted corners of the mezzanine, the wide opening of the hearth and of the window above it, which gape like two menacing mouths. This house is one of the rare modernist buildings which can rival the titanic ambience of the Mannerist palaces or of Richardson's Ames pavilion (1880), one of the most remarkable buildings of the nineteenth century. But two astonishing roofs in the shape of flying saucers lift it out of the world of the cave; by their sheer contrast with the walls they give this building its unity and its uniqueness, a modernist application of the bridge which borders on science fiction.

Wright's most directly dual-natured building was also one of his most famous successes, Fallingwater. The client, Edgar J. Kaufmann,

the proprietor of a department store in Pittsburgh, was very receptive to Wright's ideas (and to his vision); in 1934, he had partly financed the designs and the travelling exhibition dedicated to Broadacre City. Built in a wooded valley in Pennsylvania, Fallingwater has a plan which is strictly regulated by the right angle. It does, however, more or less fit into a triangle so as to hold on to the three elements of its setting: the hillside, the waterfall and the river. The house comprises a huge living room on the ground floor and four bedrooms, each one extended by a private balcony which is larger than the room itself.

Approaching the house after several hours' travelling, we see it first from the small bridge over the river. The noise of the waterfall is all around, but the water beside the house is calm like a deep reservoir. The parapet of the bridge echoes those on the two wide balconies which soar out from the house; the bridge is an integral part of the house. There is a wide straight roof slab perpendicular to the bridge. Under this runs a balcony, first parallel with it, then suddenly taking off and bursting forward over the water. Between this and a balcony beneath, a glass pavilion overlooks the site. Suspended from the lower balcony, a hanging staircase descends towards the river and ends in a small landing just above the water. The walls of the house, like the ruin of a monumental mole, once again take up the romantic masonry of Taliesin; they seem to belong to the nature of the place while the horizontal plateaux symbolize the abstract world created by man. The overhead trellis, another bridge image, also becomes visible as we approach, at first near the entrance, creating an illusory porch, then again in the pergola of the living room. The third material of the house, glass, combines the vertical of the stone walls and the horizontal of the concrete bands in various contrapuntal designs. Thirty years after the Unity Temple, Wright's architecture has become once again a sculptural creation like those books which on opening make a little paper scene. Formal abstraction dominates the buildings of the same period, the major exceptions being the E.A. Smith plan (1938) and the Hanna house of Palo Alto (1937). The 'abstract' houses (Jacobs, Rosenbaum, etc.) like the more rough and primitive houses (Pauson, Pew, etc.) are all geometrical compositions made up of parallel plateaux and vertical planes. Fallingwater adopts the more complex device of the Prairie houses but instead of two rectangular volumes intersecting at right angles it has three, stacked one above another, which contrast vividly with the vertical elements; the set-off between them creates a vaguely pyramidal silhouette and a lively sensation of movement. The deliberately emphasized sense of volume and thickness of these geometrical slabs accentuates the paradoxical character of this extraordinary building.

Top: the Kaufmann
house, 'Fallingwater',
Bear Run, Pennsylvania,
1935–6. In the
foreground, the parapet
of the entrance bridge.
Bottom: the Miller
house, Charles City,
Iowa, 1946.

MOBILIS IN MOBILE

[1] 'The large central room
... looks like a lovely grotto
lit mysteriously from above,
and inhabited by a forest of
graceful stalactites'. Peter
Blake, concerning the
Johnson Wax Building
(p. 100).

[2] 'The tenuous, open steel
frame of these tall buildings
is, in character, the very
reverse of feudal masonry
mass.' *Autobiography*,
p. 316.

The grotto is a homogeneous image which is the simplest composite of the cave and the bridge. It is an artificial cave, not buried but constructed – in this it belongs to the world of the bridge – it possesses the full range of qualities of the two worlds of which it is the synthesis. Its possibilities range from the smooth and metallic, all shining curves, to the rough, dry and angular.[1] Like the ruin, the grotto is above all an image of the cave together with superficial features of the world of the bridge. The only real homogeneous blend, the bearer of a rich, clearly defined imagery, we will call the *Nautilus*.

Although his houses, and Taliesin in particular, had the distinctive features of this new 'archetype', it was much more obvious in Wright's designs for office blocks. Amongst the small number of buildings described in the autobiography – clearly those for which he had a particular fondness – three of them fully realize this synthesis of metal and the cave which is the *Nautilus*. The first was the Larkin Company Administration Building, in Buffalo N.Y. (1904), which placed Wright immediately among the pioneers of the architecture of the twentieth century. The second, the Glass Skyscraper for the National Life Insurance Company, in Chicago (1924) was not built. The third and last was one of Wright's most famous buildings, perhaps the definitive building if one must be chosen, and paradoxically one of those furthest from the stereotyped idea that is held of his buildings: the S.C. Johnson & Son Company Administration Building in Racine, Wisconsin (1936–39). Although the autobiography does not even mention Fallingwater, Wright devotes several pages to each of these three projects, as well as to the house built in 1938 for 'Hib' Johnson, the proprietor of the Johnson Wax Company.

The new archetype this time shows the possibilities in the exploitation of metal.[2] A watertight cave, the *Nautilus* bore the stamp of that modernity which, in the last years of Wright's life, sometimes tipped over into science fiction. Buildings such as the Friedman house, the Guggenheim Museum, the Kalita Humphrey theatre (1955–59), the Greek Orthodox church in Milwaukee (1956–61), the Beth Sholom synagogue (1954–59) and the Marin County Civic Center (1957–62), which each in its own way demonstrates a rather 'cartoon-style' futurism, only partially avoided this temptation, whose apogee was reached in the designs for Broadacre City with its flying saucers, (1943–58), for Pittsburgh Community Center and suspension bridges (1947), for the 'One Mile High' skyscraper for Chicago (1956), and even for the Huntingdon Hartford Play Resort for Hollywood (1947).

The *Nautilus*, as Verne described it, combined four special features. The first was its extraordinary nature: mysterious and formidable like the unknown inhabitants of the marine depths, a 'manmade

'EAGLEFEATHER'

FOR MR AND MRS ARCH OBOLER   LOS ANGELES
                FRANK LLOYD WRIGHT   ARCHITECT

Interior of the Larkin Building, Buffalo, New York, 1903–4. Following double page: Johnson Wax Company, Racine, Wisconsin, 1936–9. Left: annexes and laboratory tower. Right: main office, interior and exterior view.

[1] Verne, *20,000 Leagues Under the Sea*, new unabridged edition, 1977, p. 58.

[2] The One Mile High tower totally contradicted Wright's penchant for the horizontal; but in fact what Wright really could not bear were half-measures.

[3] JV, p. 64.

[4] V., p. 66.

[5] V., p. 77.

[6] R. Banham, *The architecture of the well-tempered environment*, London, 1969, 1984, in particular chapters 3, 4 and 5.

[7] *Autobiography*, p. 150.

[8] As Banham remarks, it was not actually what might be described as an air-conditioning system, like those which Willis Carrier was developing at the time (R. Banham, pp. 86–92, 175).

[9] *Autobiography*, p. 256.

[10] *Autobiography*, p. 257.

phenomenon'.[1] Wright was undoubtedly fascinated by the spectacular. This seems to be more true for the later works[2] but it may also be detected even in the impressive perspectives of the Larkin Building, in the internal spaces full of visual surprises in the Prairie houses or even in those overhangs which so intrigued the first readers of the Wasmuth monographs. Just as spectacular – in the primary sense of the word – were the extravagant Midway Gardens, the Imperial Hotel and the Maya houses.

The second characteristic of the boat, the watertight seal, is essential for its survival. The seal of the *Nautilus* was so absolute that its doors were invisible,[3] so complete that even the language spoken by its crew was completely indecipherable.[4] In his steel plate, hermetically sealed cell,[5] Professor Aronnax observed that ventilation was a major problem; Reyner Banham, by studying in minute detail the role of ventilation in modern architecture,[6] recognized the Larkin Building as one of the first whose architecture took air-handling into account. In order to protect the interior from noxious gases blown out by the trains which ran along beside the building, its exterior was 'a simple cliff of brick, hermetically sealed'.[7] The working plans were already prepared when the idea occurred to move the four distribution staircases to the outside of the main volume, and also to combine these with service ducts. Fresh air from intakes at the top of the four corner stair towers was piped to the basement, where it was cleaned and heated, although there was no humidity control.[8] The air was circulated to each level by a network of vertical ducts in the columns surrounding the central atrium, and distributed through ventilation grilles under the balcony fronts and ceiling beams. Extracts on the external walls collected the foul air and returned it to the basement, where it was expelled, again at the four corners of the building.

The Johnson Wax Building was also hermetically sealed.[9] Like the Glass Skyscraper for National Life Insurance, whose surfaces were 'opalescent, iridescent copper-bound glass',[10] it had had a kind of glazing whose effect was to *visually* enclose the space. Manufactured from tubes of Pyrex glass produced specially for the building – as in Captain Nemo's vessel, which for reasons of secrecy was built at several points around the globe – the glass of the Johnson Wax building does not allow a view from the outside: it only reveals its striated, marine and decorative substance like the diaphanous membranes of jellyfish. The striations recur all over the building, from the refined grilles of the lift cages to the cupola over the publicity department, and surmounting the walls whose brick courses and stone trim persistently stress the horizontal. These striations reinforce the curves and countercurves which the right-angled projections emphasize even further; they are

Opposite: the living room of the Friedman house, Pleasantville, New York, 1949–50. Pages 122 and 123, top: the Llewellyn Wright house, Silver Springs, Maryland, 1953. Page 123, bottom: the Friedman house. On the left, the car port.

Page 124: 'the red square', Wright's 'signature'. Page 125, top: entrance to the Morris shop on Maiden lane, San Francisco, 1946–8. Bottom: the Walker house, Carmel, California, 1948.

Page 126, top: the cupola of the Guggenheim Museum. Bottom: interior of the Beth Sholom synagogue, Elkins Park, Philadelphia, 1959. Page 127: detail of the arrises of the synagogue.

perfectly at one with the overall concept of an 'aerodynamic' building, with supple and fluid forms like 'a woman swimming naked in a stream, cool, gliding, musical in movement and in manner.'[1] This sense of movement not only derives from a play of circular designs and cylinders, it owes a great deal to the total harmony throughout the building's features and volumes. No other building by Wright belonged to this extent to the smooth and dynamic aesthetic of the world of metal. The laboratory tower, built a few years later, picked up these characteristics, as did 'Wingspread', the house built for 'Hib' Johnson, whose central wigwam was pierced by a metal spiral staircase leading to a belvedere; its restrained appearance completed the 'machine-like' ambience produced by the smooth brick, the arched plywood and the mechanically repetitive clerestories.

[1] Editorial in the May 1938 issue of *Life Magazine*, quoted by Wright (*Autobiography*, p. 470).

EVERYTHING THROUGH ELECTRICITY

What made possible the building of the *Nautilus*, the effortlessness of its movement and its absolute airtightness, was electricity, a discovery new to architecture, an ethereal energy of huge potential. Verne entitled a chapter in his book 'Everything through electricity'. It was certainly electricity which created companies such as Johnson Wax and the Larkin Company and which made possible buildings of great height such as National Life Insurance. Unlike most architects, Wright knew how to achieve an artistic effect from this new thing. By night, the nature and the shape of the windows still further enrich the strange elegance of the Johnson Wax building.[2]

Wright described the Larkin Building as the 'genuine expression of power directly applied to purpose in the same sense that the ocean liner, the plane or the car is.'[3] The building was completely fitted out with many inventions and designs of Wright's own – except for telephones and waste paper baskets for which, to his great displeasure, 'the office had already done the necessary . . ., all the rest was part of the building or had been designed with it'. Even the parts of the building were rethought in the same spirit: 'the top-story was a restaurant and conservatory . . . the roof was a recreation ground paved with brick.' We find the same architectural innovations as those proposed twenty years later by Le Corbusier, but, unlike all the other precursors or imitators of the turn of the century, Wright wanted an architecture which was 'practical in all its details', 'the authentic expression of a power directly applied for an objective'.

The National Life Insurance project, twenty years later, continued the 'war machine' spirit: 'These pylons are continuous through all floors . . . and enlarged to carry electrical, plumbing, and heating conduits which branch from the shafts, not in the floor slabs at all but all in piping designed into visible fixtures extending beneath each ceiling

[2] 'By its whiteness and its intensity, I recognized the electric light which surrounded the submarine boat with so magnificent a display.' (Verne, p. 64).

[3] *Autobiography*, p. 151.

Marin County Civic
Center, San Rafael,
California, 1957.

to where the outlets are needed in the office arrangement. All electrical or plumbing appliances may thus be disconnected and re-located at short notice with no waste at all in time or material and are free of the building in vertical shafts.'[1] The Glass Skyscraper was in effect a real vertical submarine, efficient, self-sufficient and perfectly organized.

[1] *Autobiography*, p. 257.

THE MONASTERY

These three major buildings where I feel we see the masked face of the *Nautilus* were all buildings intended to be used as offices, but their design, as well as the nature of their clients, made them more like *unités d'habitation*, to use Le Corbusier's term. Wright thought that the Johnson Wax building inspired work like a cathedral inspires worship. Because of the introverted nature of the building and the company life it sheltered, Kelly Smith suggested replacing this analogy with that of the monastery.[2] He recalls the Johnson Wax television show for Christmas 1956, during which a procession of robed employees carrying altar candles and singing carols slowly traversed the galleries of the building. The company was closer to the paternalistic models of the end of the nineteenth century than to the forces dominating the industrial world of the 1930s. At Racine Wright encountered the same ideal of the integrated collective life as that which inspired his own community, the Taliesin Fellowship, which he founded in 1932.[3] At the opposite end of the scale to the giant corporations of American industry of 1936, the Johnson Wax Company allowed him to realize his ideal of an office block 'on the small scale' and to declare the power of this type of establishment to reunite human beings in an ordered, productive collaboration.

For the Taliesin Fellowship, a refuge and place of certainty for the believer, Wright drew up rules which were clearly monastic: 'our home life must be simple. Meals in common. Fixed hours for work, recreation and sleep. Each worker will have his own room for study and rest . . . The Farm and the Garden will be so managed to employ the help of the apprenticeship so that a substantial portion of the living of members may come from their own labor on the ground.'[4] Within this 'active confraternity', the apprentices would have direct experience of manual labour: to the basic essential of work on the land was added the production of furniture, pottery, glass and weavings, fulfilling 'a primary requirement . . . to engage in all the daily work of necessary Fellowship maintenance', not to mention its construction![5] And if entertainments were organized – plays, concerts, films, picnics – they were arranged by the Fellowship, on its own grounds. The monastic rule had become less rigid but life was no less self-sufficient.

[2] Norris Kelly Smith: *FLW a study in architectural content*, New York, 1966. Note that the palace of the Dalai Lama at Lhassa was the only building which was not signed by Wright to be displayed on the walls of the studio at Taliesin during the 1950s.

[3] Cf Martin Pawley, *FLW – Public Buildings*, London, 1970 (pp. 14–16).

[4] *Autobiography*, p. 392–94.

[5] It was not unheard of for the apprentices to finish off the building of houses for which the costs could not be completely covered by the client.

Design for the 'Glass
Skyscraper' of the
National Life Insurance
Company, Chicago,
1924. Not built.

Even more successfully than the Johnson Wax Company, Taliesin thus made a reality of the fourth virtue of the *Nautilus*, cultural self-sufficiency, both economic and social. From the very beginning, that is twenty years before the founding of the Fellowship, Taliesin had been envisaged as a refuge which would ideally be self-sufficient. 'The place was to be self-sustaining if not self-sufficient, and with its domain of two hundred acres as to be shelter, food, clothes and even entertainment within itself. It had to be its own light-plant, fuelyard, transportation and water system.'[1]

[1] *Autobiography*, p. 171.

Resembling the beautiful living room at Taliesin, Captain Nemo's cabin was 'a large rectangle with canted corners, ten metres long and six wide by five high. A luminous ceiling, adorned with delicate arabesques, cast a clear and gentle light over this museum and all its marvels. For a museum it truly was, and in it a lavish and intelligent hand had assembled all the treasures of nature and art, displaying them in the same artful disorder that we find in a painter's studio.'[2] The ultimate interior, shaped as if by natural forces, Nemo's cabin was in perfect taste, at once artistic and bourgeois, like the interiors which were designed in every detail by Wright, for example the Morris shop in San Francisco (1948). The shop is almost concealed behind a brick wall, which encroaches over and partially blocks the single opening, the entrance archway – almost a porthole – whose architectonic design shows both archaism and genius in its play of overhangs and recessed areas;[3] the interior, smooth and curvilinear, is dominated by an extraordinary luminous ceiling made of bubbles and bulbs. The Guggenheim Museum developed the same theme on a different scale – but it does not equal the shop's success as one of Wright's most perfect achievements.

[2] Verne, pp. 91–2.

[3] Presumably these covings are a homage to (or an exaggeration of?) H.H. Richardson, a great lover of fully centred arcs.

A gigantic *Nautilus* run aground on Fifth Avenue, the Guggenheim was already a spectacular 'museum' before the exhibits were moved in, with its strange and incongruous silhouette in the shape of a mysterious and formidable marine animal. Its principal mass, smooth and opaque, is pierced only by fine horizontal clefts. It cannot function without electricity, since a visit to the gallery begins with an ascent by lift to the summit from which one descends slowly around the gallery, by way of the huge spiral of the giant nautilus.

Like the *Nautilus*, Taliesin gradually filled up with objects recalling a time of distant voyages, stored under the great height of its ceiling and its changing plays of light. 'As work and sojourn overseas[4] continued, chinese pottery and sculpture and momoyama screens overflowed into the rooms where, in a few years, every single object used for decorative accent became an "antique" of rare quality.'[5]

[4] On the occasion of the building of the Imperial Hotel.

[5] *Autobiography*, p. 174.

During his years in Japan, Wright was asked by a wealthy Boston

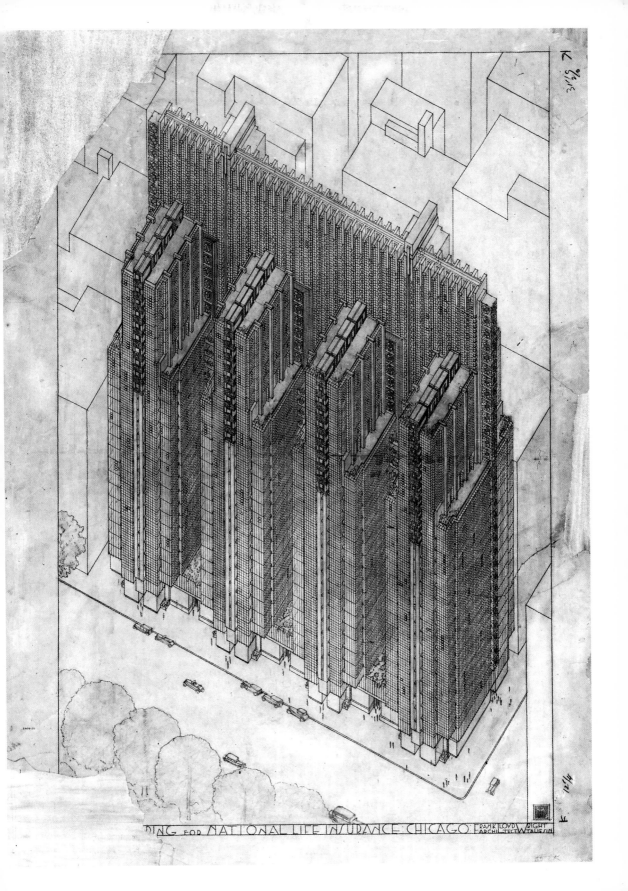

DING FOR NATIONAL LIFE INSURANCE CHICAGO FRANK LLOYD WRIGHT ARCHITECT W TALIESIN

[1] This collection is now in the Boston Museum of Fine Arts.

[2] *Autobiography*, p. 528.

family to choose and buy old woodcuts.[1] Fired by the search and by his unlimited purchasing power, he soon became an agent for other private collectors and also for the Chicago Art Institute and the Metropolitan. In spite of the enormous sums spent, Wright so valued these works of art that in the end he admitted that the deal was a scandal, as the Orient was being deprived of treasures beyond price that were its rightful property. 'I grew ashamed of it finally'.[2] But in the great hall at Taliesin, amongst the 'antiques of rare quality' to which a few animal skins add a barbarous odour, we are far from the ideal Japanese interior which is empty, save perhaps for humblest practical objects: a rake, a broom, a straw mattress, a kettle . . .

Wright on site at the
Guggenheim Museum.

Further reading

Ausgeführte Bauten und Entwürfe von FLW, Wasmuth Portfolio, Berlin 1910 (new American edition, 1963, 'FLW, Buildings, plans and designs').
Ausgeführte Bauten von FLW, Wasmuth monograph, Berlin 1911 (new American edition, 1968, 'The early work').
H.T. Wijdeveld, *The life-work of the American Architect FLW*, Wendingen monograph, 1924–25 (new American edition, 1965).
H.R. Hitchcock, *In the nature of materials*, Hitchcock monograph, New York, 1942.
G.C. Manson, *FLW to 1910: the first Golden Age*, New York, 1958.
V. Scully, *FLW*, New York, 1960.
P. Blake, *FLW: Architecture and Space*, New York, 1960, Baltimore 1964.
H. Jacobs, *FLW: America's Greatest Architect*, 1965.
R. Banham, *The Architecture of the Well-tempered Environment*, 1969, 1984.
B. Zevi, *FLW*, 1979, bilingual German-French edition, 1981.
E. Tafel, *Years with FLW – Apprentice to Genius*, McGraw Hill Book Company, New York, 1979; Dover Publications, New York, 1985.
B.B. Pfeiffer, *FLW drawings*, Tokyo, 1984–85.
J. Lipman, *FLW and the Johnson Wax Buildings*, Rizzoli, New York, 1986.
C.R. Bolon, R.S. Nelson and L. Seidel, *The Nature of F.L.W.*, University of Chicago Press, Chicago and London, 1988.

ARTICLES
R. Mac Cormac, 'The anatomy of Wright's Aesthetic', *in Architectural Review*, 1968, no 852.
J. Castex and Ph. Panerai, 'La logique de l'espace chez Louis Kahn et F.L. Wright', *in Neuf*, Brussels, Sept./Oct. 1970.
D. Hoppen, 'A journey with Frank Lloyd Wright into Architecture', *in U.I.A. International Architect* no 6/1984, London.

FROM THE WRITINGS OF F.L. WRIGHT
Art and Craft of the Machine, lecture published in the catalogue of the fourteenth annual exhibition of the Chicago Architectural Club, Chicago, 1901.
The Japanese Print, an Interpretation, Chicago, 1912, new edition of 1967.
In the cause of Architecture, series of articles republished by F. Gutheim, *FLW's Historic Essays for Architectural Record, 1908–1952*, New York, 1975.
An Autobiography, 1932, 1943, French edition: 'Mon autobiographie', Paris, 1955.
Selected Writings, 1894–1940, collected by F. Gutheim, New York, 1941.
The future of Architecture, 1953, French edition: 'L'avenir de l'architecture', Paris, 1966.
The Natural House, New York, 1954, London, 1971.
A Testament, New York, 1957.

Chronology

1869
Frank Lloyd Wright was born on the 8th June at Richmond Center (Wisconsin), the son of a preacher, William Wright, and Anna Lloyd Jones. The Wright family left Wisconsin for Iowa and for Rhode Island (1871).

1874
The Wright family set up home in Weymouth (Massachusetts).

1876
Wright's mother came across Froebel's educational games at the Philadelphia Exhibition.

1877
The family returned to Madison, in Wisconsin. For six years, Wright would work during the spring and summer on his Uncle John's farm.

1885
After his father's departure in this year, Wright studied civil engineering at Madison University and was a part-time designer with the engineer A. Conover.

1887
Wright left Madison and his family to go to Chicago. He became a designer with L. Silsbee then went to work for Adler and Sullivan.

1889
Wright married Catherine Tobin; he was assigned all residential design in the Adler and Sullivan practice and built his Oak Park house.

1893
Break with Sullivan; at 24 Wright opened his own practice.

1901
First of the 'Prairie house' series.

1909
In spite of success and intense productivity (over 130 buildings) Wright broke with his surroundings; he abandoned his wife, children and studio and left for Europe to prepare the Wasmuth Monographs (1910–11) in the company of Mrs Cheney. Wright was 40.

1911
Back in the United States, Wright founded 'Taliesin'.

1914
First fire at Taliesin; Mrs Cheney was one of the six people who died. Taliesin II was built.

1915–21
Visit to Japan in the company of Miriam Noël, his second wife, in order to build the Imperial Hotel (the only building in Tokyo which remained intact after the earthquake of 1923). Back in the United States, Wright spent most of his time in Southern California (the 'Maya houses', 1921–23).

1924
Separation from Miriam Noël (divorce in 1927).

1925
Second fire at Taliesin; construction of Taliesin III. Publication of the Wendingen monograph. Wright met 'Olgivanna'.

1932
Transformation of the Wright practice into a school of architecture, 'Taliesin Fellowship'. First edition of the autobiography.

1936
At 67 Wright built his two most famous projects, Fallingwater (Kaufmann house) and the Johnson Wax Company offices (approximately his 210th building). Beginning of the series of Usonian houses.

1938
Start of the construction of Taliesin West, in Arizona.

1943
Second revised edition of the autobiography. Great post-war activity frequently using ideas conceived during the 1920s.

1959
On the 9th April, at almost 90 years of age, Wright died, leaving more than 400 buildings.

Picture credits

Anderegg-Hoppen
38b, 39a, 101, 128

Collection PPP
9, 11a, b, 23a, 29a, 49b, 54, 55, 79a, 89a, 109a, 111, 133, 134

Christián Devillers
33a, 97, 99b

Frank Lloyd Wright Memorial Foundation
12, 13, 14, 17, 23b, 24b, 25a, b, 46, 51b, 71b, 83, 95b, 108, 115b, 131

Hedrich-Blessing
19a, 115a

Donald Hoppen
84, 85, 86

Johnson Wax Company
31, 118, 119a, b

Françoise Labbé
57

Alan Levitt
113a

Philippe Moreau
25b, 33b, 34, 35a, b, 36, 38a, 39b, 63a, b, 77, 98, 99a, 100, 103b, 104

Museum of Modern Art, New York
16, 43a, 44, 53b, 66, 68, 95a, 117

Roger-Viollet
20, 29, 41b, 93a

Guy Rumé
121, 122, 123a, b, 126a, b, 127

Daniel Treiber
58a, 59, 60, 61a, b, 62, 74, 75, 102, 103a, 124, 125a

Cover
Preview at the Guggenheim Museum, New York, Fifth Avenue. PPP photo collection.

Acknowledgements

This study was begun in 1974, at the request of Henri Bonnemazou, whom I thank. I also thank the friends who helped me source the illustrations: Christian Devillers, Donald Hoppen, Françoise Labbé, Alan Levitt, Philippe Moreau, Guy Rumé, Valérie Vaudou.

Index

Numbers in *italics* refer to picture captions

DATE DUE

SEP 3 '96 S		
SEP 1 1 PAID		
DEC 12 96 S		
DEC 1 2 1996		
NOV 19 '97 S		
NOV 2 4 PAID		
OCT 05 '04 S		
SEP 0 7 2004		
GAYLORD		PRINTED IN U.S.A.